Advanced Introduction to Freedom of Expression

Elgar Advanced Introductions are stimulating and thoughtful introductions to major fields in the social sciences and law, expertly written by the world's leading scholars. Designed to be accessible yet rigorous, they offer concise and lucid surveys of the substantive and policy issues associated with discrete subject areas.

The aims of the series are two-fold: to pinpoint essential principles of a particular field, and to offer insights that stimulate critical thinking. By distilling the vast and often technical corpus of information on the subject into a concise and meaningful form, the books serve as accessible introductions for undergraduate and graduate students coming to the subject for the first time. Importantly, they also develop well-informed, nuanced critiques of the field that will challenge and extend the understanding of advanced students, scholars and policy-makers.

For a full list of titles in the series please see the back of the book. Recent titles in the series include:

Advanced Introduction to

Freedom of Expression

MARK TUSHNET

William Nelson Cromwell Professor of Law, Harvard University, USA

Elgar Advanced Introductions

 **Edward Elgar**
PUBLISHING

Cheltenham, UK • Northampton, MA, USA

Published by
Edward Elgar Publishing Limited
The Lypiatts
15 Lansdown Road
Cheltenham
Glos GL50 2JA
UK

Edward Elgar Publishing, Inc.
William Pratt House
9 Dewey Court
Northampton
Massachusetts 01060
USA

A catalogue record for this book
is available from the British Library

Library of Congress Control Number: 2018944035

This book is available electronically on *Elgar Advanced Introductions: Law*
www.advancedintros.com

ISBN 978 1 78643 715 0 (cased)
ISBN 978 1 78643 717 4 (paperback)
ISBN 978 1 78643 716 7 (eBook)

Typeset by Servis Filmsetting Ltd, Stockport, Cheshire
Printed and bound in Great Britain by TJ International Ltd, Padstow

Contents

Acknowledgements

Frederick Schauer, Geoffrey Stone, and Rebecca Tushnet read nearly complete versions of this book and made extremely useful comments. Much of the material is the result of my efforts to make sense of free expression law for my students, who I thank for their patience.

For nearly fifteen years I have been teaching US free expression law using material prepared by Professor Stone. That material is brilliantly organized, and I tell my students that they will understand free expression law if they understand why the materials are organized as they are. Nearly everything I know about free expression law I have learned from Frederick Schauer and Geoffrey Stone, and this book is dedicated to them.

Introduction

Free expression law arose from legal efforts to control and punish speech critical of government leaders and their policies, the classical law of sedition. Over time the law expanded to deal with rules addressing not only the substance of what speakers said but how and where they said it – the law of demonstrations 'in the streets'. It also expanded to deal with speech generally – artistic expression and commercial advertising, for example – rather than only with political speech. In most jurisdictions there is today a reasonably well-developed set of rules dealing with these problems.

Scholars persistently ask whether existing doctrine, whatever it is, fits emerging problems of free expression. Today, for example, scholars ask whether the existing rules about false statements that damage reputation (libel) are well-suited to a world in which such statements are instantaneously disseminated over social media. Similarly with rules about the relation between the financing of political campaigns and the possibility of personal and institutional corruption: How should free expression law respond to what is perceived to be the effect of substantial disparities in wealth, and therefore in opportunities to engage in speech, on politics? Perhaps existing doctrine 'scales' well in the new media environment, and perhaps it is entirely suitable to deal with new problems. But, to know whether that is true it is helpful to have in hand a general framework for thinking about free expression law.

This book is designed for readers who are already familiar with basic ideas about freedom of expression. It assumes that readers are conversant with the justifications scholars have offered for giving freedom of expression robust constitutional protection – more robust than the protection given to many other activities, including the right to pursue one's chosen career. These justifications typically include: (1) the proposition that expression is distinctively important for the assertion of a person's autonomy; (2) the proposition that freedom of expression is useful for discovering factual truth and for approaching over time normatively desirable policies; and (3) the proposition that freedom of expression is essential to the maintenance of representative democracy. Further, the book assumes that readers are familiar with the general outlines of criticisms of those justifications – that many activities other than expression are at least as important as vehicles for developing one's autonomy, that sometimes the search for truth reaches its goal (the truth); that we have many variants equally entitled to be called representative democracy. For these reasons the book does not go into the justifications or criticisms in detail, although occasionally one or more justifications and critiques are mentioned in specific contexts.

The book is also designed for readers interested in freedom of expression generally, not with the treatment of freedom of expression in any individual legal system. Constitutional doctrine in the United States does play a large role in organizing the material, primarily because the US Supreme Court has dealt with freedom of expression issues for a significantly longer period than any other constitutional court (including the European Court of Human Rights), and its decisions have often been the focal point for thinking about free expression problems elsewhere. The result is that the *framework* of US doctrine is quite useful as a means of organizing the presentation, even when – as is often the case – the specific doctrines followed in the United States do not carry with them any distinctive normative value.

At the same time, the book is an *introduction*, not a comprehensive survey of all the quite interesting issues that arise in connection with government efforts to regulate or prohibit speech. It says almost nothing, for example, about whether there are reasons supporting different forms of regulation of newspapers on the one hand and radio and television on the other. The role that a speaker's motivation plays in triggering or limiting regulation is mentioned occasionally but not given systematic treatment. Each reader will almost certainly come up with other topics that he or she thinks ought to have been addressed. The book's aim is to develop a structure within which those topics might be inserted, though even here there will be shortfalls.

In thinking about free expression law we have to avoid one pitfall, while acknowledging that the concern underlying it has to be taken into account. The pitfall is in focusing on threats to free expression in authoritarian or mildly authoritarian regimes. It is not a good argument against some free expression doctrine to urge, 'Imagine what would happen if [insert the name of your favorite dictator or repressive regime] could invoke this rule.' One can usually be reasonably confident that judges in that regime would not be able effectively to invoke some doctrine limiting the government's power. So, a stringent rule designed to control repressive rulers will probably fail to do so, and might prevent non-repressive regimes from adopting sensible policies. The domain of a real law of free expression is the flawed but reasonably well-functioning democracy, with reasonably free and fair elections, opposition parties that function reasonably well, and a reasonably robust civil society.

At the same time, though, we must be alert to the possibility that a seemingly benign rule might, in the wrong hands (such as a popularly elected president with authoritarian tendencies kept in check by the political opposition and civil society), lead to a downward spiral into a truly authoritarian regime. Another risk is that a sensible rule, administered sensibly in most cases, might sometimes be administered badly, to target people who are disfavored for reasons other than their views (ethnic minorities, for example). These concerns are captured in a useful phrase, the 'pathological perspective'. That is, we should consider whether the laws we are dealing with might have been produced by a legislative process infected by something alien to a true democracy. These possibilities suggest that free expression doctrine should have a prophylactic aspect, generating doctrine that outruns its direct justification.

The book deals primarily with the *structure* of legal doctrine dealing with freedom of expression, and only secondarily and occasionally with specific doctrines and outcomes except to illustrate broader structural matters. Those doctrines and outcomes sometimes flow from institutional concerns that we can identify generically, but often they are best explained by reference to a nation's values and culture. It is widely thought, for example, that the US free expression law reflects a distinctively high degree of suspicion of government, whereas the law elsewhere is premised on greater willingness to give governing officials some leeway. These cultural observations may well be important in understanding free expression law in specific jurisdictions, but they can also sometimes be a wild card played to stop conversation.[1]

One theme deserves mention at the outset: Legal doctrine can be structured in one of two ways (a necessary oversimplification for purposes

---

1 For further discussion, see Chapter 1.

of even an advanced introduction). It might use a relatively categorical or rule-bound approach, which characterizes US law (in broad outline, though not always in every detail), or a more standards-based approach that is sensitive to a wider range of considerations, typically captured in doctrines of proportionality. The question of whether or when one or the other approach is better than another will arise recurrently, even, as we will see, when the considerations underlying the rule-based or categorical approaches can in principle be incorporated into a sensitively applied proportionality test. Again, the fact that they *can* be incorporated is different from the question of whether they *will* be so incorporated. And that latter question, and many others, can often be answered only if we pay attention to specific institutional details – whether national governance is highly centralized or decentralized, how judges are chosen and trained, and more. The upshot is that, though the book offers a general framework for thinking about issues of freedom of expression, the conclusions one draws for particular nations and problems may well vary considerably.

1 Basic concepts

1.1 Introduction

Assume that the following regulations of expression have been adopted by reasonably well-functioning and democratically representative legislatures. (Later we will consider what we should think about in determining whether a legislature is reasonably well-functioning and democratically representative.)

Banning the Indirect Encouragement of Terrorism[1]

A person commits an offense if he publishes a statement that is likely to be understood by some or all of the members of the public to whom it is published as an indirect encouragement to them to the commission, preparation, or instigation of acts of terrorism, and at the time he publishes it he intends members of the public to be indirectly encouraged or otherwise induced by the statement to commit, prepare, or instigate acts of terrorism, or is reckless as to whether members of the public will be indirectly encouraged [etc.].

Statements that are likely to be understood by members of the public as indirectly encouraging the commission or preparation of terrorism include every statement which glorifies the commission or preparation (whether in the past, in the future, or generally) of such acts, and is a statement from which those members of the public could reasonably be expected to infer that what is being glorified is being glorified as conduct that should be emulated by them in existing circumstances.

How a statement is likely to be understood and what members of the public could reasonably be expected to infer from it must be determined having regard both to the contents of the statement as a whole and to the circumstances and manner of its publication.

It is irrelevant whether any person is in fact encouraged or induced by the statement to commit, prepare, or instigate any such act.

---

1 The example is drawn from the UK Terrorism Act 2006.

An Act to Improve the Enforcement of the Law in Social Networks[2]

Service providers that operate Internet platforms which are designed to enable users to share any content with other users or to make such content available to the public with more than two million users must, within 24 hours of receiving a user complaint, remove or block access to content that is 'manifestly' unlawful. They must remove other unlawful content immediately, which is presumed to be within seven days. Unlawful content is defined through an enumeration of existing offenses making speech unlawful: Nazi propaganda, child pornography, defamation, incitement to hatred, and dissemination of depictions of violence.

Service providers must provide an easily recognizable, directly accessible and permanently available procedure for submitting complaints. Networks that receive more than 100 complaints per year must, twice a year, publish on their web-sites details of their efforts to eliminate criminal activities on their platforms, the criteria applied in content-removal decisions, the number of complaints received, and how they were dealt with. Failure to make the required reports is subject to fines up to more than 50 million euros (55 million dollars).

1.2   The *law* of free expression and reasonable legislative choices

We can take a number of approaches to thinking about these statutes. We might, for example, ask whether they are good as a matter of policy: Are they likely to produce *net* social benefits – achieve desirable social goals such as reducing terrorism and dissemination of unlawful speech without inhibiting the dissemination of socially valuable speech too much? Or, we might ask whether they are consistent with one or another theory of freedom of expression: Will they enhance democratic self-governance or individual autonomy by reducing the inhibitions that unlawful speech causes with respect to political participation or social life generally? Importantly, when we think about the compatibility of these statutes with theories of freedom of expression, we ordinarily should acknowledge that people disagree not only about whether a specific statute or proposal is consistent with some theory but also about which theory of freedom of expression is the best one available.

---

2 The example is drawn from the German Act to Improve the Enforcement of the Law in Social Networks, effective October 1, 2017.

1.2.1 The basic idea

When we consider these statutes as a matter of constitutional law, though, there is another consideration, which may be of overriding importance. Whatever *we* think of the statutes, a presumptively democratically responsible legislature has enacted them. That implies, first, that the legislature *believes* that the statute is good policy (will produce net social benefits), and that it is consistent with a theory of freedom of expression that the legislature accepts.[3]

Why should that matter? Because – deferring for a moment some collateral questions – it is one thing for each of us as individuals to come to a different assessment from the legislature's, and another thing for a court exercising the power of constitutional review to come to a different assessment. When a court does so, it is substituting its assessment – perhaps of policy, but far more likely of the compatibility with a theory of freedom of expression – for the legislature's, in a decision with real legal consequences. Put another way, the constitutional law of free expression is not (only) an exercise in political theory but is also a way of organizing the institutions of governance in a democracy.[4]

Modern constitutions of course *authorize* courts to exercise the power of constitutional review, but they do not – or at least need not be understood to – authorize them to do so merely on the basis of the judges' own assessment of a statute's policy wisdom or compatibility with the judges' preferred theory of freedom of expression. Rather, constitutions should be understood as, in the first instance, authorizing democratically representative institutions – legislatures – to make policy judgments, evaluations of theories of freedom of expression, and assessments of the compatibility of specific enactments with those theories, with courts playing a back-up role. The reason is that, within appropriate limits, democratic choices about policies that affect freedom of expression are no different from all the other choices that constitutions remit to ordinary democratic decision-making.

---

3 This book deals with the constitutional law of free expression. The idea that expression should be free (in some senses) can also support policy ideas that can inform legislation and statutory interpretation.

4 In systems of political constitutionalism, where courts do not exercise the power of constitutional review, the constitutional right of freedom of expression is 'enforced' through continuing political discourse about the meaning of freedom of expression, so the tension between the legislature's judgment and individual assessments is either substantially weaker or entirely absent. Even in such systems, though, courts might interpret statutes and the authorization of executive actions in light of their views of freedom of expression. Most of this book focuses on judicial rather than political constitutionalism, and on the capacity of courts to administer a law of free expression.

Consider a legislature that engages in an extended debate over the foundations of freedom of expression. After full debate, the legislature decides – perhaps in the course of adopting a specific piece of legislation – that the account provided by John Stuart Mill of freedom of expression as a mechanism for determining truth is better grounded than an account of freedom of expression as a distinctive vehicle for personal autonomy. Having chosen a theory of freedom of expression, it then adopts a statute compatible with that theory but incompatible with an autonomy-based theory – perhaps a ban on 'Holocaust denial'. If, as seems unquestionably true, the Millian account is itself defensible, and if – as might be more questionable – it is defensible to believe that Holocaust denial does not contribute to the identification of truth, it would be inconsistent with basic ideas about democratic self-governance for a court to step in and say that the autonomy-based theory actually provides a better basis for freedom of expression. To put the point forcefully, in the circumstances the legislature's decision to ban Holocaust denial is no different from a legislature's decision to enact a program limiting a business's ability to discharge pollutants into the atmosphere: Both rest upon reasonable but contestable judgments about the foundations of a good political order.

Of course, what the limits on legislative choice among theories of freedom of expression are matters a great deal. We can readily identify two general limits. First, there might be reasons to think that democratic representatives will not deliberate appropriately about particular types of legislation. For example, they might be acting at a time when they are especially vulnerable to distorted judgment – considering anti-terrorism legislation in the immediate aftermath of a major terrorist incident, for example. As we will see, identifying what falls into this category is a complex task.

Second, although people have reasonable disagreements about which theory of freedom of expression is the best one, and reasonable disagreements about whether a particular statute is compatible with freedom of expression, some disagreements are not reasonable – or, put another way, sometimes there is simply no reasonable way to connect a particular statute to *any* defensible theory of freedom of expression. In US constitutional law the standard here is 'mere' reasonableness or minimum rationality; in other constitutional systems the standard is the step in proportionality analysis that requires a rational connection between the statute and permissible legislative goals.

1.2.2   Some simple qualifications

The foregoing argument is about *legislative* choices. Many actions that adversely affect expression, though, are taken by executive officials – police officers arresting demonstrators, for example. Such actions typically do not have the same democratic warrant that statutes do. The officials will typically contend that some statute authorized them to take the action they did. If so, the first question will be whether that contention is correct – that is, whether the action was indeed authorized by statute. So, for example, a prosecutor charges someone with violating a law prohibiting interference with national security by publishing a statement leaked from some official within the government. The first question we should ask is not whether it is constitutionally permissible to punish someone for published leaked material, but rather whether the statute the prosecutor relies on actually covers the activity alleged to have occurred.

In answering that question, we might want courts to require that actions that adversely affect freedom of expression be explicitly authorized, or, put another way, that there must be clear legislative authorization for such actions. Such a requirement does not pose the questions about democratic self-governance that direct displacement of legislative judgments does.[5] The core question about the appropriate limits on the powers of politically responsible officials will arise in only two circumstances: (1) when the executive official's action is authorized by a statute satisfying whatever requirements of clear statement we think appropriate; or (2) when the executive official correctly claims to act pursuant to some inherent prerogative power, one that exists prior to and independent of legislative authorization. (Executive officials quite often claim that they have such a prerogative power with respect to actions that in their judgment are necessary to protect national security, but – depending on the details of specific constitutions – that claim might or might not be correct. Whether it is, is a question about what the constitution says about executive power, not – directly – what it says about free expression, although considerations of free expression might influence how we interpret the provisions dealing with executive power.)

Though the prior description of the core question relies on an open and fully deliberated legislative discussion of theories of freedom of

---

5 In federal systems one might say something similar about statutes and regulations adopted at the sub-national level, and the suggested analysis about express authorization might be invoked when sub-national rules are challenged on the ground of incompatibility with the national constitution.

expression, it is of course unrealistic to expect that such discussions will occur routinely (though, when especially important or potentially intrusive statutes are under consideration, these discussions might occur). How should we respond when the discussions have not occurred?

There appear to be two possibilities. We might uphold the legislation if reasonable legislators could have mounted a reasonable defense of a theory of freedom of expression that we impute to the statute. This is something like an 'existence' proposition: We uphold the legislation if there is an account of freedom of expression with which it is compatible, even if we have no reason to think that legislators themselves had that account – or indeed any account – in mind when they acted. We might take this course either because we think that legislators are generally well-intentioned, or because we think that the alternative course is basically pointless: If we tell legislators that they have to 'show their work', that is, make it clear that they have deliberated over basic questions, they will go through the motions, for example by commissioning reports from committees or experts laying out the constitutional arguments, without actually deliberating.

As noted, the alternative course is to require that the legislative record demonstrate real deliberation. We might think that even something as simple as having a report on constitutional matters in the legislature's hands could affect some legislators' views. Legislators who start out merely going through the motions might over time come to believe that they ought to deliberate. Still, we might worry about requiring real deliberation. The more evidence we require to ensure that the deliberation is real rather than feigned, for example, the more likely it is that we will effectively substitute our judgments for legislators' on questions about which disagreement is reasonable. And, more narrowly but also important, a requirement of real deliberation, even if satisfied by relatively thin evidence, might impose greater burdens on legislative capacity than is appropriate.[6]

1.2.3   Identifying predictable failures of deliberation

As noted, we might be reluctant to defer to legislative deliberation when we have reason to think that the legislature's consideration of the statute was distorted. Of course we cannot take our disagreement

---

6 This might be particularly true in connection with sub-national legislation.

with the legislative output as sufficient to show distorted deliberation, although it might be appropriate to use that disagreement as a signal that we should look for the possibility of distorted judgment.[7]

Determining the baseline against which 'distorted' judgment should be measured poses another difficulty. We know that much legislation today results from 'special interest' pressures. Legislators respond to the special interests of bankers to give them some exemptions from regulations applicable to stock brokers, for example. Or, to take an example from a German case, manufacturers of chocolate candy persuade legislators to ban the sale of puffed-rice candy coated in chocolate, simply to preserve the chocolate-makers' share of the candy market.

We accept this sort of special interest legislation as inevitable, and perhaps desirable, in a complex modern political system. Special interest legislation is sometimes thought problematic because it results from a distorted political process: The beneficiaries of special interest laws – the chocolate-candy makers – are said to be concentrated and able to mobilize effective political force more readily than those burdened by the legislation, here the parents who have to pay more for candy for their children. The crudest version of this is that the chocolate-candy makers can promise to make campaign contributions to legislators who vote for the restrictive legislation, and parents cannot. There are, of course, subtler versions, but they all center on the proposition that legislators vote for special interest legislation because they believe that doing so will enhance their ability to retain their seats. And, that might not be a bad thing: A legislator who loses her position cannot do *anything* to promote the public interest, and we might think that the cost of special interest legislation is offset by the benefits of having experienced legislators who can enact other laws in the public interest. Most modern and reasonably democratic political systems seem to accept special interest laws as an acceptable cost.[8]

Should we have the same view where special interests obtain legislation adversely affecting freedom of expression? Consider, for example, legislation requiring that foods produced with genetically

---

7 The discussion in this chapter deals primarily with regulations of speech based on its content. Chapter 5 deals with content-neutral regulations.

8 Some speech- and press-protecting statutes, such as laws shielding journalists from inquiries to which all others have to respond, can be seen as examples of special-interest legislation as well.

modified materials (GMOs) be labeled so that consumers can distinguish between GMO-based foods and non-GMO (sometimes 'organic') foods. At present there appears to be a scientific consensus that GMO-based foods pose no greater threats to human health than non-GMO foods. The labeling requirement might be seen as legislation serving the special interests of the organic-food sector.

Perhaps the standard for evaluating speech-related special interest legislation should be the same as that for evaluating all other forms of special interest legislation. Notably, a unified standard might not be toothless. The German Constitutional Court held the ban on chocolate-covered puffed-rice candy unconstitutional as completely disproportionate; other bases might be that it interfered with the right to pursue a lawful occupation or the right to free development of personality or, in the US system, that it was not even minimally rational. On this view, the mere fact of special interest influence on speech-related legislation does not count as a factor that distorts legislative deliberation about speech-related laws.

The proposition that a single standard should be applied to all special interest legislation poses one quite important problem. Special interests influence legislation by appealing to legislators' interests in retaining their seats. The legislators' interest in re-election, in the general context, does not count as a distortion of the political process. Indeed, one might think that nearly everything a legislator does is aimed at securing re-election. Then, though, we should consider whether that interest is problematic *outside* the context of special interest legislation. The clearest example comes from the law regulating politics itself. It is a truism in US constitutional law that legislators enact regulations of campaign finance whose effect, and often whose intent, is to make it difficult for challengers to win elections. Yet, if the interest in retaining one's seat does not count as a distortion when we think about legislation in general, should it count as a distortion with respect to some subcategory? Perhaps so, if we can find a subcategory where the self-interest is so strong that legislation based on self-interest cannot be justified even by the possibility that easy re-election will allow legislators to enact public-interest laws.[9] As noted, the best candidate for such a subcategory is the law of politics itself.

---

9 It may be worth noting that in the United States some legislators defend restrictive campaign finance laws, concededly likely to discourage challengers, on the ground that the restrictive

Another candidate for 'distortion' in the legislative process arises from the 'speech causes harm' paradigm discussed in more detail below. Sometimes legislators enact statutes aimed at reducing the risk that harm will occur. Again, the 'indirect encouragement of terrorism' statute is an example. Apply the basic argument to such a statute. The legislators have estimated how much the legislation will reduce the risk, and conclude that the reduction is large enough to justify the restriction on speech. So far so good. Suppose, though, we have reason to think that legislators have overestimated the degree to which the law will reduce the risk of harm (and, to drive the point home, that the legislators would not have enacted a law with the same impact on speech if they thought that the law would not reduce the risk enough). The circumstances occasioning the misestimation might count as enough of a distortion of the legislative process to warrant displacing the legislative judgment.[10]

A common observation is that legislators enact repressive statutes, particularly those aimed at political speech, when concern about the harm caused by the regulated speech is at a high point, often after dramatic incidents that focus citizen and legislative attention on a specific type of speech. Drawing upon modern ideas about cognitive processing – immediate or 'fast' responses contrasted with more deliberate or 'slow' responses – and a sort of intuitive 'folk' wisdom, commentators suggest that legislators are likely to misestimate risks and benefits under such circumstances. So, for example, a statute proscribing indirect encouragement of terrorism might be enacted immediately after a terrorist attack attributed to such encouragement. Prosecutors might search the statute books to find something to use against those who indirectly encourage terrorism, juries might act under heightened conditions of fear, and even judges might be over-influenced by the immediate occasion for concern.

The folk wisdom here might be correct, but we can raise some questions about the account. Most narrowly, the phenomena addressed by modern cognitive science are far removed from the legislative process: The 'fast' responses occur within seconds of the provocative event and dissipate over time, though they apparently leave some residue. Legislation that goes through ordinary or even accelerated

---

system will relieve them of the chore of raising money and thereby allow them to spend more time serving the public interest. How deferential should we be to that defense?

10 The misestimation might occur through overestimating the regulation's likely benefits as well.

parliamentary procedures is unlikely to be affected in any strong way by the 'fast' cognitive process. In addition, dramatic events that trigger legislation or enforcement of existing laws can lead to *appropriate* updating of risk estimates: Before the event, we might have thought that the risk was small that indirect encouragement of terrorism would actually lead to a terrorist attack, but now we have new information that we factor into our risk estimates. Whether a dramatic incident will lead to distorted or more accurate judgments seems unclear in general.

Most broadly, we need to consider how widespread are these distortions of legislative judgment. Suppose we think that a terrorist attack is likely to produce a worrisome distortion of judgment. Do we think the same about legislation to restrict the advertising of some product sold to consumers, enacted immediately after the outbreak of illness associated with the product?

Finally, as noted in the Introduction, courts are well-advised to take a pathological perspective when assessing speech-restricting legislation. That is, they are to ask whether this specific law – or laws dealing with this or that topic, or laws restricting speech generally – is likely to be the product of a pathological deviation from a reasonably well-functioning democracy's ordinary operation. If they are to do so, though, they must not themselves be susceptible to the pathology. This suggests, first, that the primary pathologies are going to be related to elections and representation and not, for example, the kinds of passions that pervade societies when many people believe the nation to be under real threat: Judges as well as legislators will feel those passions. We might think that judges' commitments to legality might offset such passions whereas legislators have little to offset their susceptibility to passion. Yet, in light of the fact that we are considering laws that can be defended with reasonable arguments founded in law, we might wonder how strong will be the counter-pressure exerted by legality.

How common are systematic misestimations of risks or likely benefits? This appears to be an empirical question, though, as we have seen, finding out what the facts are here as elsewhere is likely to be difficult. Probably the best we can do is rely on folk wisdom. And, notably, that wisdom might vary from one constitutional system to another. As a quite speculative example, perhaps law-makers in systems that have recently emerged from a long period of civic disorder ('post-transition' legal systems) will be better – or, alas, perhaps worse – at estimating the risks associated with speech critical of government policy than are law-makers in long-established democracies. Another example: Many scholars of free expression believe that legislators often misestimate risks and benefits when they deal with political speech. Is that equally true – or true enough – when they deal with commercial speech? Local knowledge is likely to be quite important here.

Beyond that, there is the problem of identifying the category over which we ask about misestimating risks and benefits, examined in more detail below. Do we ask whether legislators will systematically misestimate risks or benefits of laws penalizing political speech, or speech about terrorism, or speech defined as indirect encouragement of terrorism? If we use larger categories and conclude that legislators are likely often enough to misestimate risks or benefits, the more willing we will be to displace the legislative judgment – and the larger the resulting impact on democratic self-governance.

All the questions about identifying problems of misestimation raise yet another concern: Suppose there is reasonable disagreement about *whether* there is a problem of misestimation in the first place. The right way to think about this issue involves making guesses about the costs of making a mistake: If we mistakenly say there is no underlying problem, we will allow some speech to be suppressed when there is no good reason for suppression; if we mistakenly say that there *is* an underlying problem, we will interfere with the public's justifiable interest in preventing the harms associated with the proscribed speech. Of course assessing those costs in any remotely precise sense is impossible. We must rely on the informed judgments of the judges who construct free expression law – and then evaluate their performance to see if we would get better results by saying that the default assumption should be that there is (or is not) an underlying problem.

These qualifications to the basic account offer some examples of the way in which free expression law must be sensitive to questions of institutional design no less than to questions about political theory.

1.2.4   The basic idea applied to accounts of democracy and culture

We are now in a position to see why free expression law cannot resolve free expression issues by relying on accounts of democracy offered by political theorists. Reasonable theoretical accounts of democracy abound, and among them are pluralist accounts that allocate different foundational theories to different problems: Epistemic theories about the ability of democracy to produce good policy can be combined with autonomy-based theories in a larger account. Law-makers can reasonably choose one or another as they address specific problems. They might conclude, for example, that a theory focusing on the epistemic benefits of democracy is best suited for problems associated with the dissemination of falsehoods, and that a theory focusing on individual autonomy is best suited for other problems. The basic idea, that courts have no good basis for rejecting reasonable legislative choices, applies with equal force when the choices are among theories of democracy as it does when they are among specific expression-affecting policies.

The same form of argument shows that normative assessments based on culture are also problematic. Cultural arguments assert that a proposed regulation of expression is inconsistent with a nation's culture of free expression. So, for example, in holding unconstitutional a national statute making it a crime to lie about having received a military honor, US Supreme Court Justice Anthony Kennedy wrote: 'Our constitutional tradition stands against the idea that we need Oceania's Ministry of Truth.'[11] The difficulty is that national cultural traditions are almost universally complex and multivalent. Against Justice Kennedy, for example, a scholar might juxtapose Justice Louis Brandeis, who wrote in a case not involving free expression: 'Our Government is the potent, the omnipresent teacher. For good or ill, it teaches the whole people by its example.'[12] And, in some sense, the entire edifice of public education is erected on the proposition that the government permissibly disseminates its version of truth.

If a nation's culture contains competing traditions about expression, as it always will, the basic idea kicks in, with an additional twist. It may well be true that some traditions are 'stronger', in some sense, than others. In the United States, for example, an anti-regulatory cultural tradition may be stronger than a pro-regulatory one. Still, what is the basis for displacing a legislative victory by adherents to the weaker tradition? By definition, in the circumstances they happened to be politically stronger than their opponents. Why should a judicially

---

11 United States v. Alvarez, 567 U.S. 709 (2012).
12 Olmstead v. United States, 277 U.S. 438 (1928). *Olmstead* is distinguishable from *Alvarez* because the latter involved coercive government regulation of speech whereas the former involved government intrusion on privacy. The point that the cases show the existence of competing strands in constitutional culture remains valid.

enforced culture prevail over that political victory? The twist is this: Cultures change, and the political victory of the weaker tradition in the case at hand may portend – may be an indication of – a change in constitutional culture. The basic idea counsels against the use of the existing culture as an impediment to cultural change itself. (This is not to say that we cannot invoke constitutional culture to explain patterns of outcomes, and even to explain specific outcomes. The basic idea is about the normative basis for institutional arrangements.)

1.3   The 'speech causes harm' paradigm

Free expression law would not be interesting if we truly believed, as the schoolyard taunt has it, that 'Sticks and stones can break my bones but words can never hurt me.' Legislatures enact statutes regulating speech because they believe that speech causes harm – or, more precisely, in light of the preceding discussion, they reasonably believe that speech causes harm. (If that belief is unreasonable with respect to some specific matter on which legislatures act, a general prohibition on unreasonable legislative action – in the form of a general right to liberty and cognate provisions – provides a sufficient basis for invalidation; no special rule for expression is required[13].)

What are the components of the 'speech is reasonably believed to cause harm' paradigm? First, there are *types of expression*. There are many varieties of speech: the publication of academic research, public speeches and displays on billboards dealing with matters of public policy ('political speech'), advertisements for commercial products ('commercial speech'), artistic displays, and much more.

Next there are the *mechanisms* by which expression causes harm. An eloquent orator might *persuade* listeners to break the law, or *incite* them to act, where the mechanism of incitement largely bypasses the listeners' deliberative capacities. A speaker's message can *shock* listeners into attacking the speaker. Hate speech can *unconsciously condition* listeners to think less of the targets, sometimes leading to lawless action against them, sometimes leading to systematically discounting the targets' views in political discussions. The mere utterance of hate

---

13 For a useful discussion of the prevalence of the Panglossian view that speech never (or rarely) causes serious harm, see Frederick Schauer, 'Rights, Constitutions, and the Perils of Panglossism', 38 Oxford Journal of Legal Studies (forthcoming 2018).

speech diminishes its targets' civic equality. Highly sexualized commercial advertisements might have similar effects.

There may well be other mechanisms by which expression causes harm, but even this brief catalogue is suggestive. In particular, it suggests that we might have great difficulty identifying the precise mechanism by which expression causes harm. A classic example is Marc Antony's speech after Caesar's assassination, which is in form of praise of the assassins, but functions as an incitement to the crowd. The US case *Beauhearnais v. Illinois* involved the distribution of materials purporting merely to describe the prevalence of crime in the African American community, but that might have been understood as hate speech.[14] A contemporary real-world example may be the radio broadcasts in Rwanda that were held to cause genocidal attacks.[15] The specific words a speaker chooses affect the message's persuasive power. To use another classic example from US law, saying 'Fuck the Draft' is different from saying 'Abolish the Draft' or 'Resist the Draft' even if the cognitive content of the three phrases is the same. As Supreme Court Justice John Marshall Harlan put it in that case, 'words are often chosen as much for their emotive as their cognitive force'.[16] Though many accounts of why some regulations of expression are permissible and others are not depend upon the mechanisms by which expression causes harm these complexities make working the mechanisms into a legal doctrine that courts can implement quite difficult.

Finally, of course, expression causes a variety of *harms*. A false statement about a person may harm his or her reputation, leading to both intangible losses and, sometimes, tangible ones such as the loss of job opportunities. An argument that some specific law – a ban on the use of marijuana for medicinal purposes, for example – is unjustified might persuade some listeners to violate that law. An emotionally effective advertisement might lead some consumers to purchase harmful products without fully appreciating the products' risks. An insult made face-to-face might lead the target to strike back physically; so might an insult distributed through modern social media.

It is implausible to believe that a speech regulation will completely eliminate the harm at which it is aimed. Consider a statute prohibiting face-to-

---

14 Beauhearnais v. Illinois, 342 U.S. 250 (1952).
15 Prosecutor v. Nahimana et al., Case No. ICTR-99-52-T (December 3, 2003).
16 Cohen v. California, 403 U.S. 15 (1971).

face insults, aimed at the physical violence that such insults can occasion; in US law, these insults are known as fighting words. No reasonable legislator would think that passing such a statute would eliminate brawls in bars. Rather, the goal is to reduce the risk of physical harms. More generally, the 'speech causes harm' paradigm focuses on reducing the risk that the harm at issue will actually be realized. The constitutional question is then whether the regulation is likely 'enough' to reduce the risk of harm 'enough'. The scare quotes here flag, once again, the issue of reasonable legislative judgment: As observers we might think that the regulation is not likely to reduce the risk of harm by much, but how much weight should we give our judgment in the face of a legislative judgment that the regulation is good enough – has a decent chance of reducing risk by an amount worth paying attention to? The case study of sedition law later in this chapter explores this question, and others, in some detail.

Return to the statutes described at this chapter's outset. The statute banning indirect encouragement of terrorism regulates a form of political speech. The mechanism by which the speech operates is 'encouragement' of 'emulation', terms that suggests an appeal to less deliberative, more emotional capacities. The harm is terrorism – or, more precisely, an increase in the risk of terrorism. The social media statute enhances existing bans on speech because the legislature believes that each mechanism by which speech causes harm is magnified when the dissemination is scaled up through social media.

How can free expression law deal with these three components? Two seemingly different strategies are available, though as we will see they may often be roughly equivalent. The first is a 'mix and match' strategy: Identify the type of speech, mechanism, and type of harm associated with the regulation in question, and develop a rule appropriate for that combination. Under this strategy, variations in any of the components might produce different rules: One rule for political speech that harms reputation by disseminating false information, another rule for commercial speech that does the same. As will sometimes be the case, different arrays of type of speech, mechanism, and type of harm can generate similar rules, but the similarity results from independent consideration of specific arrays, not from the dispositive role of any one feature. With important qualifications to be discussed soon, this corresponds roughly to the strategy underlying US law.

Most other constitutional systems pursue a seemingly different strategy, ordinarily described as a structured proportionality analysis. In this strategy, the three components are taken into account, but variations in the array do not trigger the deployment of different rules. Rather, structured proportionality directs analysts to fold the components into a unified analysis, which – foreshortened here – asks whether the restriction of expression is adequately justified by the degree to which the relation advances permissible public interests. The answer to that question will depend upon the array of the components, which is why, in practice, the approach underlying US law and structured proportionality may not be dramatically different.

One question pervades the 'speech causes harm' paradigm: How finely grained should the description of the components be? If the harm is law-breaking, should it matter that one regulation is aimed at preventing looting, another at preventing littering? If the type of speech is commercial, should it matter that one regulation is aimed at tobacco advertising, another at high-sugar drinks? Subject again to the possibility that after analysis one might end up with identical rules for cigarette advertising and soda advertising, it would seem that a fully rational system would indeed go through separate analyses rather than lumping both regulations into the category 'regulations of commercial advertising'.

Yet, the more finely grained the analysis, the more complex the overall system becomes.[17] An omnicompetent decision-maker (familiar in the legal literature as Ronald Dworkin's Judge Hercules) can work with a system as complex as one can imagine. Less capable decision-makers, which is to say all real-world ones, will not do as well. The problem can be seen best from the perspective of a judge in a nation's highest constitutional court. She may be confident that she can deal with a complex system, but she may and probably should believe that judges below her in the hierarchy cannot. And, she may and probably should understand that she will not be able to review every decision those judges make. From her perspective, those judges will make many irreversible mistakes as they try to implement a complex system. Better, she might think, to give those judges a simple system to implement – not a finely grained one, but one that groups phenomena that are rationally distinguishable into larger categories. With such a system, the judges will make fewer mistakes overall (again, from the higher court judge's perspective). The system will produce some 'mistaken' decisions because the categories are imperfect, but – the judge might

---

17 In other domains of constitutional law the difficulty goes under the heading 'the level of generality problem' or the issue of rules versus standards.

think – the reduction in unreversed lower court decisions will exceed the mistakes induced by the rough categories.

Were a judge to accept this argument, she might sometimes find herself in a difficult psychological position. Suppose that the highest constitutional court determines that, taking all regulations of commercial advertising into account, the best way to deal with that category is to require the government to demonstrate a strong connection between its regulation and the reduction in the harm the advertising causes; the subject-matter of the advertising is irrelevant. Allowing lower courts to uphold regulations based on their evaluation of the seriousness of the harm averted will produce too many irreversible errors. Suppose a lower court judge *correctly* implements the system with rough categories, for example by finding unjustified a regulation of advertising for high-sugar sodas because the government could not make a strong connection between the regulation and the reduction of childhood obesity. But, the higher court judge might think, the problem of childhood obesity is serious enough to support regulations with a 'moderately strong' connection to obesity-reduction. In a finely grained system, the judge could reverse the lower court decision. Doing so, though, would increase the system's complexity and thereby induce new errors. The conclusion is that the higher court judge should strike down a regulation that she believes to be adequately justified, to preserve an overall *system* of freedom of expression that works better than one with an 'exception' for soda advertising. We should not be surprised if judges were to find this conclusion uncomfortable – and if, as a result, they pushed for an increasingly fine-grained approach.

Several features of the foregoing argument should be noted. First, the argument for less finely grained descriptions is an institutional one, focusing on the hierarchy of decision-makers and the capacity of higher-level ones to review decisions below. Second, the argument is deeply empirical, though the facts on which it relies are undoubtedly difficult to determine reliably. We might make some stabs at intuitive judgments about the facts: The institutional argument is more likely to be accurate with respect to larger categories than smaller ones, for example. And, systems that generally produce higher quality judges throughout the legal system might be better able to handle the more finely grained approach.

Third, the argument is that something short of a completely fine-grained approach – a system that replaces focus on everything presented by a case with some rougher categories that group facts together – may be the best way to implement a legal system of freedom of expression. But, nothing in the argument tells us *what* categories are the right ones. The US approach is highly categorical, separating the types of speech into only three categories. To oversimplify, political speech receives the highest level of protection, commercial speech a moderate level, and sexually explicit speech a relatively low level. A common criticism of the US system is that these categories are too rough, and in particular that they are insensitive to the mechanisms by which speech in the three categories causes harm. One could agree with that criticism and still defend a rather categorical approach – more finely grained than the current US approach, but well short of an approach that attempts to take every feature of a case into account.

1.4   Categorical rules and proportionality

As already noted, the US law of free expression is much more categorical than the law in most other jurisdictions, although perhaps not as categorical as sometimes asserted. It is usually said that US law deploys three categories when dealing with regulations of speech based on content.[18] There is 'high-value' speech, whose core is speech on matters of public interest ('political' speech), but which encompasses a much wider set of expressions; there is 'intermediate-value' speech, primarily commercial speech defined as product and similar advertising – and not much else; and there is 'low-value' speech, a grab-bag of topics such as obscenity and libelous statements.[19] In US law, once we determine whether a regulation deals with high, intermediate, or low-value speech, we then apply distinctive tests.[20] The test for determining the constitutionality of a regulation of high-value speech is, roughly, whether the regulation serves an especially strong or 'compelling' public interest, and does so in the narrowest possible way (the latter requirement so that the regulation does not penalize speech that is actually valuable). The test for intermediate value is, again roughly, whether the regulation serves an 'important' public interest, and does so in a way that is reasonably well 'tailored' to that interest, the latter

---

18 For alternative and perhaps descriptively more accurate characterizations, see Chapter 3.3.

19 Chapter 4 discusses an alternative, and more perspicuous, account of 'low value' speech, as expression that falls outside the 'coverage' of free expression law.

20 The verbal formulations of each test vary from case to case, and these variations may reflect subcategories within larger ones.

requirement meaning that the regulation need not be the best imaginable way of promoting the public interest but must be a reasonably good one in light of available alternatives. And, finally, the test for low-value speech is that the regulation is a minimally rational way of advancing some permissible public interest. But, especially in connection with low and intermediate value speech, institutional concerns about how the regulation will actually be implemented can lead to the invocation of rules that restrict government power more than the stated doctrine suggests.

This doctrinal structure reflects skepticism in US law of content-based regulations. That skepticism, though, places pressure on that very structure because, as is obvious, the distinction *among* types of speech based on their value appears itself to be content-based. The result is that US law tends to assimilate all speech into a single category subject to a single test, typically the stringent one applied to political speech. One manifestation of this phenomenon is a group of decisions giving extremely narrow definitions of intermediate and low-value speech, whose effect is to push the speech at issue into the high-value category. So, for example, low-value speech includes obscene material, but US law defines 'obscenity' so narrowly that a great deal of quite explicit and highly sexualized material is not obscene – and is as a result treated as high-value speech.[21] Similarly with false statements: Only false statements that cause material harm, such as commercial fraud or libelous statements that injure reputation, are low value. Other false statements, such as Holocaust denial, are high-value because they do not cause material harm. The US Supreme Court held unconstitutional the so-called Stolen Valor Act, a statute making it a crime for a person falsely to claim that he or she had received military honors; an important component of the Court's analysis was that such false statements did not ordinarily result in material harm.[22]

Notably, the tendency to define the intermediate-value and low-value categories narrowly and the high-value category expansively results in outcomes that for many are manifestly unsuitable. The best defense of such results relies on the institutional argument outlined in the

---

21 United States law distinguishes between low-value obscenity and what has come to be described as a broader category of 'pornography'. Obscene material is a subset of pornographic material, but US law treats non-obscene pornography not involving children as (in general) falling within the high-value category.

22 United States v. Alvarez, 567 U.S. 709 (2012).

preceding section: Given the characteristics of the US legal system, a strongly categorical approach – three or even only one – is the best one available.

There is, of course, another doctrinal structure available, widely used throughout the world though at least formally rejected in the United States, in connection with high-value speech. The alternative is structured proportionality analysis, which is typically described as having a four-step sequence. The first three steps have analogues in US law, though they have quite different content in proportionality analysis. A preliminary inquiry is whether the challenged legislation 'infringes' a protected right, here the right of free expression but sometimes relevantly a general right to liberty or a right to free development of personality. The test for infringement is quite weak, asking only whether the regulation adversely affects those seeking to exercise the right. Proportionality analysis then kicks in, to determine whether the infringement is justified.

The first step asks whether the regulation purports to advance some permissible public purpose. This requirement is typically easy to satisfy, certainly in the context of the 'speech causes harm' paradigm; all that is needed is the identification of some harm, generously understood, at which the legislation is aimed. Consider the US Stolen Valor Act: At step one, a proportionality analysis would ask whether a person's false claim to have received a military honor might cause some harm. The prime candidate, offered by the US government defending the statute's constitutionality, was the public interest in preserving the integrity of the system of military honors: False claims to have received such an honor might lead to general public skepticism about the value of those honors, thereby diminishing the honor associated with true claims. Under most accounts of proportionality, that interest would count as a harm, the reduction of which is a permissible public purpose.

The second step in proportionality analysis asks whether the regulation advances the public purpose. Here too the test is quite weak. Verbal formulations vary, but their core idea is that the second step is satisfied if it is reasonable to think that the regulation might reduce the targeted harm.

Proportionality's third step asks whether there are less restrictive alternatives to the challenged regulation that would achieve the public purpose. At this point formulations and applications of the requirement matter quite a bit. In the 'speech causes harm' paradigm, content-based regulations are almost always designed to reduce the risk of harm, not to eliminate the harm completely. When considering whether there is a less restrictive alternative to a challenged regulation, we have to ask whether we are looking for an alternative that reduces the risk of harm exactly as much as (or, though given legislators' incentives this is unlikely, more than) the challenged regulation does. In general it seems quite unlikely that there would be such alternatives, so the 'less restrictive alternative' step probably involves looking for an alternative that reduces the risk of harm less than the regulation does, but not too much less. Yet, this formulation poses rather directly the basic question of displacing reasonable judgments by democratically responsible legislatures.

Another issue arises at the third step. Although proportionality analysis usually identifies a single public purpose and looks for less restrictive alternatives that achieve that purpose, legislation typically advances two or more purposes: Reduce the risk from indirect encouragement of terrorism without authorizing excessively intrusive surveillance of speakers, for example, or reduce the threat to the integrity of the military honors system without incurring excessive costs associated with alternatives. Alternative policies that are less restrictive with respect to one purpose might be more restrictive with respect to another. If one defines the problematic speech associated with terrorism more narrowly than indirect encouragement, for example, public authorities might have to dispatch more personnel to listen to questionable speeches and might have to investigate more intrusively. The less restrictive alternative to a criminal ban on false claims about military honors might be maintaining a centralized list of all those who have received such honors, but doing so might be quite costly and unproductive in view of how infrequently such false claims are made.

Proportionality analysis has some resources to deal with the issue of multiple purposes. It might require that any alternative be less restrictive with respect to all purposes; it might rule out administrative costs as a justification for choosing one regulation over an alternative that is less restrictive with respect to the regulation's 'core' purpose. Whether these resources are sufficient to answer the basic question is uncertain.[23]

---

23 The issues associated with this step in proportionality analysis arise whenever it is used, not only in connection with freedom of expression.

Proportionality's final step is proportionality 'as such' or *sensu stricto.* Here one asks whether the incremental achievement of the regulation's purpose is justified taking into account the incremental reduction in freedom of expression. We can understand this step better by initially, and somewhat misleadingly, asking whether it is different from an extremely finely grained 'all things considered' balancing of competing interests. Several examples can frame the inquiry. In *Debs v. United States*, Eugene V. Debs, a prominent leader of the American Socialist Party, made a speech to a large audience in which he severely criticized the use of the military draft during World War I.[24] In *Abrams v. United States*, several radicals threw from the roof of an apartment building in New York some leaflets opposing US intervention against Russian revolutionaries.[25] A completely finely grained analysis would take into account the fact that Debs was a major figure in left-wing politics, who had received almost 6 percent of the votes cast for the presidency in 1912, while the defendants in *Abrams* were people Justice Oliver Wendell Holmes called in dissent 'poor and puny anonymities'. In both Germany and the United States, important free expression cases have arisen from public demonstrations conducted on symbolically important days: the anniversary of the death of Rudolph Hess and Good Friday, respectively.[26] The demonstrators chose those dates in part because they believed that their message's impact would be enhanced by its association with the dates. Suppose similar cases arose but the demonstrators chose the dates randomly or simply for convenience. A completely finely grained analysis would take into account the different roles the specific dates played in the demonstration.

Truly case-by-case balancing and completely finely grained approaches are impossible as legal doctrines.[27] Neither can provide the guidance a legal doctrine must provide to subsequent decision-makers. Still, one can move quite far in the direction of completely finely grained analysis if one wants. For purposes of planning an appropriate system of crowd control, it certainly matters whether a planned demonstration is likely to attract an audience of 20 rather than 100. After the event, it might make a difference that a demonstration involved 50 people rather than (even) 100, for example. And one can imagine scenarios in

---

24 Debs v. United States, 249 U.S. 211 (1919).

25 Abrams v. United States, 250 U.S. 616 (1919).

26 1 BvR 2150/08 (the *Wunsiedel* case); Shuttlesworth v. City of Birmingham, 394 U.S. 147 (1969).

27 They may be appropriate in one's ordinary life, as one considers how to assess one's own or others' actions, but law has an institutional structure that moral evaluation does not.

which it might matter – with respect to the risks posed by using different techniques of crowd control, for example – that the demonstrators
were wearing shorts rather than long pants.

What is working here, of course, is some notion of relevance. Who the
speakers were, the dates of the demonstrations, the crowd size, even
the demonstrators' attire – all might be taken into account if they are
relevant to determining whether (in the present context) a regulation
is proportionate *sensu stricto*. The key point, though, is that 'relevance'
singles out categories of facts associated with the problem: It might be
relevant that the demonstration occurred on a specific date, but it is
unlikely in the extreme that it will be relevant that they arrived at the
venue in cars rather than buses.

Proportionality analysis is therefore categorical to some extent, though
perhaps less categorical than the US approach. Considering the basic
question about overriding reasonable legislative judgments leads to a
further narrowing of the differences between proportionality and the
US approach. We must make some seemingly normative judgments at
proportionality's third and fourth steps – whether the proposed alternative is truly less restrictive with respect to all permissible purposes
and whether the incremental burden on speech is justified. The basic
question arises when our normative judgments on those questions
differ from those imputed to the legislature.

Robert Alexy, one of proportionality's most learned defenders, offers
an analysis that reduces the occasions on which judges will end up
enforcing their normative views against the legislatures'. He proposes
to divide statutes and justifications into three groups each. Some regulations infringe on freedom of expression, but only to a 'low' degree,
some infringe on it to a 'high' degree, and others fall in the middle.
Similarly, some justifications are intrinsically strong, others intrinsically weak, yet others are of moderate strength. For Alexy, regulations
that are low in adverse effect and are supported by a strong (and perhaps even by a moderate) justification are presumptively valid, and
the presumption is rarely overcome. Similarly, regulations with a high
adverse impact and supported by a weak justification are presumptively unconstitutional.[28] For present purposes the precise contours
of Alexy's proposal are irrelevant. What matters is that his scheme
of proportionality has moved quite a long way from a finely grained

---

28 From a US perspective, one might regard regulations of this sort as (almost) irrational.

analysis to one with nine largish categories. Such a system is more finely grained than the US one with three categories, but we are no longer in an entirely different conceptual universe.

The distance between the US approach and proportionality is reduced even more by the presence within the US approach of exceptions to the categorical approach. Sometimes these exceptions are seemingly ad hoc, sometimes they might rest on relevant differences and for that reason establish a new category within the US analytic system. The US Supreme Court upheld a city zoning regulation that confined bookstores selling sexually explicit but not obscene books and films to a relatively small and commercially unattractive area. Two assumptions lay in the background: that the city could not single out ordinary bookstores for similar special treatment, and that sexually explicit but non-obscene material is covered by the First Amendment.[29] Those assumptions ordinarily would lead to the conclusion that the Court should apply the stringent test to regulations of high-value speech. Instead, the Court held that a zoning regulation of 'specified sexual activities' (the term used in the zoning ordinance) would be tested against a looser standard – as later articulated, that the regulations served a 'substantial government interest' and that 'reasonable alternative avenues of communication remained available'.[30] This case illustrates either a purely ad hoc exception or, more plausibly, the creation of a new, rather small category encompassing only zoning regulations dealing with businesses engaged in the dissemination of sexually explicit but non-obscene material. The more such exceptions there are, the more similar the US system comes to proportionality analysis in its fundamental structure, though not in the language describing the structure.

The US approach, though, generates another question, one that need not be asked within proportionality analysis. If ad hoc exceptions or small categorical exceptions can in principle be created, why not create a new exception whenever a new problem arises? The US Supreme Court has noticed the question, but has not offered a decent answer. The Court upheld statutes making it a criminal offense to produce child pornography, defined as a form of sexually explicit material involving children that did not satisfy the Court's definition of

---

29 See Chapter 4 for a discussion of the latter point.
30 Young v. American Mini-Theatres, 427 U.S. 50 (1976); Los Angeles v. Alameda Books, 535 U.S. 425 (2002).

obscene material prohibitable as such.[31] Its explanation was that the very production of the material involved an independent crime, child abuse, and that having a market for such material provided an incentive to produce it, that is, to abuse children sexually. Drawing upon that rationale, Congress enacted a statute prohibiting the production of material depicting animal cruelty. Defending the statute, the government pointed out that animal cruelty was itself illegal, so that the production of the banned material necessarily involved an otherwise illegal activity, and that the existence of a market for these depictions provided an incentive to produce it and thereby commit the crime of animal cruelty. Yet, despite the analogy, the US Supreme Court held the statute unconstitutional.[32] Its analysis was largely historical, asserting that there were only a few categorical exceptions to the requirement that regulations of high-value speech be subject to a stringent test and that it would not establish any new ones. Yet, the distinction the Court drew between the animal cruelty statute and the newly created category for child pornography was thin to the vanishing point.[33]

The more categorical approach taken in the United States and the proportionality approach taken elsewhere can converge, and to some significant degree have done so. Obvious differences remain, perhaps most notably with respect to so-called hate speech, substantially regulated everywhere but the United States, where nearly all regulations of such speech are unconstitutional.[34] The reasons for that difference, and perhaps most others, may lie more in institutional and cultural concerns than in legal analytics.

1.5   Sedition law as a case study

The development of the law of sedition – punishment for speech critical of government policy – illustrates many of the themes introduced in this chapter. Both historically and today, governments, even

---

31 New York v. Ferber, 458 U.S. 747 (1982).

32 United States v. Stevens, 559 U.S. 460 (2010).

33 The only analysis relevant to this issue was that *Ferber* 'grounded its analysis in a previously recognized, long-established category of unprotected speech', which is true only if 'grounded' means 'more or less related thematically' to obscene material. The animal-cruelty statute was aimed at what is generally known as 'crush porn', suggesting that it too could be said to be similarly grounded.

34 R.A.V. v. City of St. Paul, 505 U.S. 377 (1992). For additional discussion of hate speech, see Chapter 4.

reasonably democratic ones, have perhaps understandably succumbed to the temptation to punish speakers who criticize government policy. Sedition law was the origin of much theorizing about freedom of expression, and – independent of that law's contribution to our understanding of the foundations of free expression law – many analytic matters lie along the path of its development.

1.5.1   The basic problem

Not surprisingly, rulers often do not like to be criticized. When they move against their critics, though, they do not ordinarily rely solely on the mere fact of criticism. The reason lies in the 'speech causes harm' paradigm: They must identify some public harm caused by speech critical of government policy. Yet, it is quite easy to do so. Criticism of a government policy (one that is constitutionally valid in itself) increases the probability that that policy will not be implemented with complete effectiveness. A pamphlet that backs up its assertion that the military draft is unjust increases the probability that some reader, persuaded by the argument, will refuse to submit to the draft. Even more, when one person asserts that the military draft is unjust and another asserts that, though all existing laws are just, it is morally permissible to refuse to comply with unjust laws, the latter's statement *also* increases the risk that someone will refuse to submit to the draft.

Sedition law, then, gets started when a government contends, typically not without basis in reason, that speech increases the risk that some valid law will be violated – in brief, that speech causes the harm of increasing the risk of law-breaking. Historically, this position generated the 'bad tendency' test: Speech could be punished if it had the tendency to increase the risk of law-breaking. As jurists considered sedition law in light of principles of free expression, they came to see that the 'bad tendency' test failed to take seriously enough the distinctive interests associated with freedom of expression.

1.5.2   The development of the US law of seditious speech

Justice Oliver Wendell Holmes, Jr., saw the problem of seditious speech through the lens of the common law of criminal attempts. Consider someone who sells rat poison to a person who plans to use it to kill a business rival. The sale itself increases the risk of criminality and so could be said to have a bad tendency. One could rely upon the good sense of prosecutors and jurors to refrain from convicting the seller of attempting to commit murder (or of abetting that crime).

The common law went further, though. To oversimplify: It imposed an intent requirement. A person could not be convicted of attempting to commit a crime after doing something that increased the risk that the crime would occur, unless he or she intended that increase in risk. The intent requirement was not terribly stringent. A person was said to intend the natural and probable consequences of his or her action. Still, the rat poison seller could not be said to intend murder as a natural and probable consequence of *every* sale.

The common law imposed another requirement. Holmes used the example of the rat poison's purchaser, who does intend to commit murder. But, Holmes offered, suppose the person sits at home thinking about committing the murder, gets into her car to drive to the rival's office, but changes her mind along the way and turns around. The common law rule was that she had not attempted to commit murder. What was required was a 'dangerous proximity to success'.

Holmes saw that the simple 'bad tendency' test applied to seditious speech was anomalous: A person could be punished for seditious speech with a bad tendency, whereas the rat poison purchaser could be punished only if she intended murder and came close enough to committing it. The constitutional protection afforded to speech required that seditious speech that increases the risk of law-breaking be protected at least as much as actions that increase the risk of murder.

Initially the US Supreme Court, in opinions written by Justice Holmes, incorporated the common law requirements with little modification. A speaker could be punished if she intended that law-breaking result from her speech, with 'intent' defined as the natural and probable consequences of her speech. And, she could be punished only if the circumstances were such as to present a 'clear-and-present danger' of law-breaking. 'Clear-and-present danger' was defined in a way perhaps not reflecting the ordinary meaning of its component words. For Holmes, whether words posed a clear-and-present danger was a question of 'proximity and degree', as in the common law of attempts.[35] Importantly, the questions of intent and clear-and-present

---

35 Schenck v. United States, 249 U.S. 47 (1919).

danger were to be decided by properly instructed juries. And, jury decisions were not immune from review, though the standard of review tilted toward upholding verdicts: Sometimes convictions for seditious speech could be overturned if no reasonable jury could have concluded that the speech posed a clear-and-present danger (again, on analogy to the law of attempts, if no reasonable juror could have concluded that the speech had a dangerous proximity to successful law-breaking).[36]

The next step built upon statutory limits on criminal liability. The US Supreme Court's initial confrontations with sedition law involved prosecutions for offenses like obstructing the draft. Those offenses identified what the Court called 'substantive evils' – breaking specific laws – and the analogy to the law of criminal attempts was reasonably straight-forward. A few years later the Court dealt with statutes identifying particular forms of speech – statutes making it a crime to advocate criminal anarchy or criminal syndicalism. The theory underlying these statutes was similar to those dealing with substantive evils: Speech falling within the statutes' scope had a tendency to increase the risk of law-breaking. The prosecution had an easier task in the criminal anarchy cases, though. Rather than showing that under the circumstances the words posed a clear-and-present danger of law-breaking, it had to show only that the words fitted the statutory definition of criminal anarchy.

In the first cases dealing with criminal anarchy statutes, the Court recognized that they posed a different problem and refrained from applying the clear-and-present danger test.[37] Instead, it paid close attention to the statutory definition, which proscribed speech that 'advocates, advises, or teaches the duty, necessity or propriety of overthrowing [the] government by force or violence'. As Justice Edward Sanford emphasized: 'The statute does not penalize the utterance . . . of abstract "doctrine" or academic discussion having no quality of incitement to any concrete action. It is not aimed at mere historical or philosophical essays. It does not restrain the advocacy of changes in the form of government by constitutional and lawful means.' These qualifications were important because they preserved a wide range of speech advocating *changes* in government policy and indeed in the form of government itself – speech that had to be protected if people were to be self-governing in any real sense.

---

36 For this qualification, see Justice Holmes's dissent in Abrams v. United States, 250 U.S. 616 (1919).
37 Gitlow v. New York, 268 U.S. 652 (1925).

Next the Court transformed these statutory limits into constitutional ones, and in time came to enforce the limits quite robustly, defining 'teaching abstract doctrine' broadly. In the course of doing so, it almost incidentally took the clear-and-present danger test as applicable to all prosecutions for seditious speech, and perhaps more important began to focus rather closely on the precise words that were said to cause the increase in the risk of law-breaking. Judge Learned Hand had proposed a word-focused approach early on. He was concerned that a clear-and-present danger test, even if administered more vigorously than the Court did, still left too many openings for officials – prosecutors, juries, and judges – to overestimate the risk that law-breaking would occur. The circumstances surrounding prosecutions, he worried, would distort judgments about risk. That distortion could not occur if the test focused solely on the words used. Higher courts initially rejected Hand's proposal to limit liability to words that 'directly . . . counsel or advise' law-breaking, but his word-focused approach eventually prevailed.[38]

After a false start in reformulating the clear-and-present danger test as one requiring consideration of 'the gravity of the "evil" discounted by its improbability',[39] the Court in *Brandenburg v. Ohio* eventually settled on the currently governing standard offered as a restatement of the clear-and-present danger test but actually a substantial reformulation. Under *Brandenburg*, speech that advocates violence or law-breaking can be punished only if it is 'directed to inciting or producing imminent lawless action and is likely to incite or produce such action'.[40] The test appears to be conjunctive: an intent element ('directed to'), a focus on words ('inciting or producing'), a temporal element (imminence), and a requirement of a close causal connection between the words and the evil to be averted ('likely to incite or produce'). This combination of features resulted from institutional considerations – that all the relevant actors were likely to overestimate the risk that speech would cause law-breaking.

---

38 Masses Publishing Co. v. Patten, 244 F. 535 (S.D. N.Y. 1917).

39 Dennis v. United States, 341 U.S. 494 (1951). The reformulation was a mistake because it allowed the suppression of speech where the evil, though unlikely in the extreme to eventuate, was regarded as extraordinarily serious, a judgment that was subject to the usual distortions of judgment under pressure.

40 Brandenburg v. Ohio, 395 U.S. 444 (1969).

1.5.3   Some observations about the US law of sedition

The US law of sedition incrementally came to offer substantial protection for speech said to cause law-breaking. First came the 'bad tendency' test in prosecutions of radicals during World War I and the ensuing 'Red Scare'. Then came a series of cases dealing with the Soviet-dominated Communist Party, articulating a somewhat stronger test. Finally, there were prosecutions associated with protests against US involvement in Vietnam, at which *Brandenburg* was aimed (even though it was a case not about anti-war protests but about a demonstration by the Ku Klux Klan). Many of the advances have a striking retrospective character. That is, the Communist Party cases of the 1950s seemed to assume that the Court had applied too loose a standard in the World War I cases, and *Brandenburg* seemed to assume that the same had occurred in connection with the Communist Party cases.

This suggests that the problem of distorted judgment may be pervasive. As seen from the 1950s, the Court in the World War I cases overestimated the risks of law-breaking, and as seen from *Brandenburg* so did the Court in the Communist Party cases even as it modified sedition law. One possibility is that distorted judgments are inevitable. We come to see that we have made mistakes in the past because our judgment then was distorted, and we correct those errors. But, in doing so, we make new ones because our judgment is now distorted in new circumstances. *Brandenburg* itself stands today as a counter-example, but perhaps in the next round of cases addressing substantial questions about seditious speech we will come to think that *Brandenburg* too was mistaken – probably in the direction of providing too much protection for speech that increases the risk of law-breaking. The 'indirect encouragement of terrorism' statute might serve as a case to test our current assessment of what kinds of speech regulations are consistent with freedom of expression.

Concerns about administering the tests for constitutionality arose at each step in the development of the law of seditious speech. Judges worried about how to ensure that prosecutors, juries, and lower court judges would make decisions providing adequate protection for expression, with adequacy measured by the Supreme Court's own assessment. The candidates included prosecutorial discretion, jury decisions controlled by instructions and subject to review on the basis of a failure of reasonableness, a focus on words to screen out distortions induced by consideration of surrounding circumstances, and a requirement of a tight causal connection between the speech and law-breaking. Notably, one institution is almost necessarily left out of this account – the Supreme Court itself. The sequence of errors corrected but followed by new errors suggests that the justices themselves can be affected by distorted judgments. Yet, there appears to be no effective way to prevent such distortions except perhaps a public discourse that insists that Supreme Court justices have a great deal of fortitude in defense of free expression.

In offering his words-focused approach and the incitement require-ment, Learned Hand observed that '[w]ords are not only the keys of persuasion, but the triggers of action'. *Brandenburg*'s incitement test might be thought to allow punishment only for words that, viewed simply as words and without consideration of their context, trigger action – that is, where the mechanism of causation is not persuasion but some bypassing of conscious deliberation. As noted earlier, such an approach might let the clever inciter go free. Perhaps that is an acceptable cost of the approach, but it is a cost nonetheless. More, sometimes we can identify people who persuade others to break the law and seem at least as culpable as the law-breakers. As Abraham Lincoln put it: 'Must I shoot a simple-minded soldier boy who deserts, while I must not touch a hair of a wily agitator who induces him to desert?'[41] Focusing solely on words of incitement might both over-protect and under-protect speech.

Requiring a close causal connection between speech and ensuing harm seems appropriate in light of historical experience. Requiring that the temporal connection be as tight as the word 'imminent' suggests might not always be appropriate. The *Brandenburg* requirement may reflect a rather high degree of self-confidence about the ability of the US political and social system to absorb shocks caused by dissident speakers. That self-confidence might have been justified in 1969, but times change, and we must be alert to the possibility that the political and social system has become more fragile. If that occurs, perhaps it would make sense to allow punishment of speech, whether inciting or persuasive, that is likely to cause unlawful action in the relatively near future. A formulation by the Supreme Court of Israel, that there be a 'probability . . . amounting almost to a certainty', might be better, or perhaps even too stringent in some fragile democracies. That may

41 Letter to Erastus Corning, June 12, 1863.

be all the more true of nations whose political and social systems are undoubtedly fragile.[42]

Constitutional courts around the world now appear to have converged on something like the US approach to seditious speech. They often use the phrase 'clear-and-present danger', though they may use it differently from the way it is or was used in US law. They tend to require a close causal connection between speech and law-breaking, though not perhaps as close as the 'imminence' standard in the United States. And, consistent with the sensibility associated with proportionality, they tend to take the circumstances in which the words were used into account more than US law does. The role that distorted judgment plays in the law of seditious speech suggests that the US approach, which 'categorically' screens out consideration of circumstances, may be better than proportionality here (and perhaps elsewhere).

---

42 For the 'probability' test, see Kol Ha'am Co. v. Minister of Interior, H.C.J. 73/53 (Isr.). The contrary view is far more widely held, with commentators insisting that quite robust protections of free expression are particularly valuable in fragile democracies. See, for example, Samuel Issacharoff, Fragile Democracies: Contested Power in the Era of Constitutional Courts (New York, Cambridge University Press, 2015); Timothy Garton Ash, Free Speech: Ten Principles for a Connected World (New Haven: Yale University Press, 2016).

2 Justifications for regulating speech

2.1 Direct and indirect justifications for regulating and protecting speech

The literature on freedom of expression is dominated by exercises in political theory (in addition to expositions of free expression law in particular jurisdictions and on specific topics). Scholars ask what free expression contributes to maintaining and deepening democratic self-governance. With those accounts in hand, scholars then ask what kinds of regulations are compatible with them. Sometimes, of course, the accounts point in different directions: A regulation compatible with a 'discovery of truth' account might be incompatible with an autonomy-based account. Theorists hope either that one account has greater force than others or that the accounts will converge rather than diverge in the large bulk of cases. Their writings tend to vindicate that hope either by presenting one account as clearly superior to alternatives or by arguing that a challenged regulation is permissible or impermissible under any account.

Political theories of free expression come in many variants, which poses an additional difficulty. Consider accounts in which free expression contributes to the development and maintenance of a healthy system of democratic self-governance. What constitutes a healthy democracy is itself a deeply contested question. Is a democracy healthy only when large numbers of people actively participate in politics or, more narrowly, vote? When does a low level of participation indicate satisfaction with how things are going; when does it indicate alienation from the political system? To know whether a regulation is consistent with or incompatible with democratic self-governance, we would have to agree on a definition of the latter. And, even more, the array of regulations of expression in a polity might be thought to be an important element in constituting that polity's understanding of what democracy *is*.

The regulation of campaign finance presents this difficulty in an especially acute form. As a first cut, we might conceive of democracy as requiring the widest possible participation in the choice of those who govern us, and of participation as involving primarily active campaigning for candidates, discussions of candidates both face-to-face and on social media, and similar activities in which citizens are actively involved in campaigns. Holding that view, legislators might enact campaign finance regulations that sharply restrict paid advertising and monetary contributions to candidates, believing not unreasonably that too many citizens would be discouraged from active participation when they observe money flooding into political campaigns. Alternatively, we might conceive of democracy as requiring sensitivity not only to votes but also to the intensity with which citizens hold their views and that the amount of money one is willing to spend on politics is a rough measure of the intensity of one's views. With that understanding legislators might enact campaign finance regulations that allow quite substantial expenditures in support of candidates and political platforms.

Restrictive and generous campaign finance laws each can reflect a coherent account of democracy. The implication from the 'basic idea' identified in Chapter 1.2.1 is probably that, to the extent that free expression law rests upon ideas about democratic self-governance, it must accept whichever choice the legislature makes. We might think that empirical questions arise within each account. The infusion of large amounts of money into campaigns might not discourage active participation much, for example. Or, having quite generous contribution limits might not measure intensity well in light of disparities in wealth whose effect is to allow relatively rich people to express intensity through contributions but not poorer people, who lack money to contribute. Clearly, though, these are contestable empirical claims and, again under the 'basic idea', any reasonable legislative assessment of the facts should prevail.

On the account developed here free expression law has little to say about what we might think are central questions about democratic self-governance even though we are assuming for the moment that free expression law exists to vindicate democratic self-governance. To put the point perhaps more strongly than it should be: How can we know whether a campaign finance statute is consistent with democratic self-governance if free expression law precludes us from choosing among available conceptions of democratic self-governance? The point almost certainly generalizes to all laws regulating the democratic political process. And, as we will see in Chapter 3, that category might reasonably be thought to encompass an enormous range of statutes. At the most general level of all, we can note the irony of invoking democracy as a basis for invalidating laws produced by democratic processes.

The account has another important feature: Once a set of laws regulating politics is in place, it will create or at least reinforce the version of democratic self-governance the laws are designed to protect. A set of laws that rests upon ideas about active citizenship will make practically unavailable the alternative of an intensity-based politics, and conversely. By having little to say about what visions of democratic self-governance are compatible with freedom of expression, free expression law ends up ratifying whatever vision happens to prevail when important democracy-shaping laws are enacted. That is an uncomfortable conclusion for many scholars, who believe that free expression law has some purchase on these questions (beyond the purchase provided by the requirement, not distinctively associated with free expression law, that the legislature's vision of democracy and its empirical assumptions be reasonable).

One might think that the line of argument just developed is confined to democracy-related accounts of free expression law. It is not. The same kind of argument can be constructed in connection with autonomy-based and truth-seeking accounts of that law. Having done so, we will find that we will be unable to defend or challenge any legislation by relying directly upon political theories of free expression.

Indirect or second- and higher-order arguments may be more promising. Chapter 1 laid out a second-order argument, there labeled 'institutional', for preferring a relatively categorical structure of free speech doctrine to a proportionality structure because doing so produces the best set of outcomes overall, taking correct and unreviewable incorrect decisions into account. Second-order arguments, with a similar focus on institutional performance, are available in connection with many far more discrete problems.

2.2   The 'chilling effect' and the constitutional law of libel in the United States

The increasing awareness of the prevalence of widely disseminated 'fake news' and of its adverse effects on democratic politics brings home the truth that there is no *social* value in the dissemination of falsehood. John Stuart Mill argued that the 'collision' of truth with falsehood would lead to a 'clearer perception and livelier impression of truth', but the context of that assertion was a discussion of political opinion, not factual truth. It is difficult to see how refuting – again and again – the claims of Holocaust deniers or flat-Earthers produces a 'clearer perception and livelier impression' of the relevant truths.

Autonomy-based accounts of free expression might protect at least some lies – think here of the fictional Baron von Munchausen, who constructed his persona around telling outrageous lies. Once again, though, we should keep the basic idea in mind: A reasonable legislature could choose the Millian account of free expression's value over autonomy-based accounts, in the context of lies.

If, on a Millian account, the dissemination of falsehood has no social value, we might think that legislators ought to be allowed to make unlawful the dissemination of whatever lies they think worth attending to. We know, of course, that there are many lies that are too unimportant for legislators to worry about, and they rarely will. Situations are readily imaginable, though, where a problem associated with lying becomes so widespread that it is worth addressing. Consider here the possibility that résumé fraud is such a situation. Résumé fraud involves false statements that pose a risk of what the US Supreme Court calls 'material harm': A person might be hired for a job that he is unqualified to perform, with bad effects for his employer and for consumers.

Should a legislature be allowed to impose liability simply for disseminating a false statement that causes or has the risk of causing material harm? One way to begin answering that question is to think about whether a legislature could be suffering from distorted judgment when enacting such a statute. Because disseminating falsehoods typically has no (or quite little) social value, the only real issue is whether the legislature might be overestimating the social benefit of suppressing some specific falsehood.

The US Supreme Court explored the problem of imposing liability for false statements in connection with cases in which public figures claimed that the dissemination of false statements about them caused material harm to their reputation – libel cases, in short.[1] The central

---

1 The US constitutional law of libel has features other than the one examined here; those other features are discussed in Chapter 4.

difficulty is easy to state. If we were confident that our institutions reliably identified as false only those statements that actually were false, we would have no problem with imposing liability for disseminating false statements. The difficulty is that our institutions are imperfect. Judges and juries, and even organizations of 'media watchdogs' supported by the media themselves, will sometimes err, identifying as false a statement that actually is true. (In the present context, errors in the other direction, identifying as true statements that are actually false, has no impact on the analysis. That form of error is important, though, when we revisit libel law in Chapter 4.) Given the risk of error, publishers will publish only material that they are confident decision-makers will find to be true, and, importantly, will refrain from publishing material where the risk of erroneous labeling is small. That will deter them from publishing some material that is actually true. Two phrases in US law capture the phenomenon. Publishers will 'steer clear of the forbidden zone'. The possibility of error causes a 'chilling effect' on decisions to publish. So, although there is no social value in publishing falsehoods, there is a social cost to imposing liability for publishing at least some falsehoods – the cost associated with forgone publication on true statements.

The solution is straight-forward: Do not allow liability merely for publishing a false statement that causes material harm such as damage to reputation. Precisely what should be substituted for such liability is a matter of judgment about which constitutional systems differ. One obvious possibility is to require that the plaintiff show falsity rather than placing the burden on the defendant to prove truth. Another is to limit liability to cases in which the defendant had some sort of culpable mental state: liability for disseminating a statement knowing it to be false (lying, in a reasonably straight-forward sense), or for doing so without paying attention to whether it is true or false ('reckless disregard of truth or falsity', the definition in the US law of 'malice'), or negligent failure to comply with applicable professional norms (a widely proposed standard). Another approach, also taken in US law, is to limit the amount of compensation available even if the substantive liability standard is met: damage to reputation from falsity might not be presumed but could be proven, and limited to actual harm. The choice among these and other possible methods of limiting liability for disseminating false statements will depend upon how large the chilling effect is thought to be. As hinted at in some cases from Australia and New Zealand, that judgment itself might depend upon one's sense of how responsible the media targeted for libel suits are likely to be: If one thinks that a nation's media tend to be irresponsible 'scandal sheets', one might allow liability for negligent failure to comply with the professional standards of responsible journalism, whereas if one thinks that the media are generally responsible one might allow liability only for reckless disregard of truth or falsity, the US approach.

The 'social network liability' statute described in Chapter 1 clearly raises 'chilling effect' concerns. Under the statute, liability is triggered by the dissemination of statements that are made unlawful by other statutes. Operators of social network must 'take down' such statements upon notification. Assume that Holocaust denial is unlawful (and permissibly so). A social network operator receives a complaint that it has disseminated something the person submitting the complaint describes as Holocaust denial. The social network must take the statement down immediately if it is 'manifestly' unlawful, and take it down shortly if it is (merely) unlawful. It is not difficult to imagine circumstances in which the complaining party describes the material as manifestly unlawful Holocaust denial, the social network's operator concludes that it is not even Holocaust denial much less manifestly so, and – importantly – that the final decision-maker concludes that the complaining party was correct. The possibility of that scenario will chill the operator, leading it to take down challenged material out of concern that the ultimate decision-maker will mistakenly disagree with the operator's correct evaluation of the material's lawfulness.

Several notes on the chilling effect in conclusion. Presented here in the setting of false statements, the chilling effect pervades free expression law. Legislatures enact statutes infringing on free expression – have an adverse effect on it – either because they suffer from distorted judgment, misestimating the social harms and benefits of the speech they target, or because they believe that the legislation promotes some public good by suppressing socially undesirable expression such as falsehood. Libel law does not appear to be an area in which distorted judgment occurs at the legislative level. The possibility of distorted judgment at that level, though, does not automatically lead to the conclusion that the legislation is justified. The reason is that distortions can occur at the level of implementation.

Even legislation that reflects an accurate assessment of social harm and benefit will sometimes miss its target, that is, will be applied to expression that does not impede that public good. The reason is that every institution applying the law in specific instances will make mistakes, and in doing so will deter people from engaging in *other* expression that similarly does not impede the public good. That is, all laws adversely affecting free expression have a chilling effect in a world of imperfect institutions. As with libel law, substantive doctrines should be developed to best promote the public good by suppressing only as much expression as is necessary to reduce the amount of socially undesirable expression (falsehoods, in the libel context, other forms of such expression in other contexts) to an acceptable level. The language of minimal impairment in proportionality analysis can be drafted into use here: At the level of implementation, libel law should minimally impair free expression.

Second, different *forms* of regulation might chill speech more (or less), though developing a metric for measuring the chilling effect might be difficult. One might think that potential criminal liability would have the largest chilling effect, for example, but perhaps the threat of large monetary liability would be more chilling to media organizations than the threat of small criminal punishments of their reporters or editors. Some critics of the stringent US doctrine requiring knowledge of falsehood or willful disregard thereof have suggested that the target of a false statement should be able to obtain a judicial declaration that the statement was false, without accompanying monetary compensation. Their thought is that the declaration would vindicate the target's interest to some extent while having a smaller chilling effect on publishers. An indication of the difficulty in devising a metric for the chilling effect is that publishers have responded to such suggestions with the argument that a declaration of falsehood would damage their reputation so much that the chilling effect would be as substantial as the imposition of monetary liability.

The 'social network' law adopts another strategy to reduce the chilling effect. Rather than impose liability for allowing criminal speech on social networks, the law requires that such speech be taken down relatively quickly. Social networks do face some financial risk – but not from failing to determine correctly that the speech should be taken down because it is criminal. Rather, the liability is imposed for failing to have in place a system for implementing 'take-downs'. The thought here is that social networks might have difficulty in determining whether a post involves criminal speech, and in particular might worry that a later decision-maker might conclude (correctly or mistakenly) that the speech was criminal and impose liability for continuing to post the material. The chilling effect of liability for posting would be substantial. In contrast, the statute could impose liability for failing to have a system in place for determining whether criminal speech was posted; presumably there would still be some risk that liability would flow from a mistaken decision that the system was inadequate, but perhaps the chance that such a mistaken decision would be made is small enough to reduce the chilling effect. Note that the point of this exercise is not to establish that a take-down system has a smaller chilling effect than criminal or monetary liability, but rather to lay out the way arguments about institutional details can be made (and can matter).

Finally, it is not clear whether proportionality analysis can be fully responsive to concerns about chilling effects. The reason is that incorporating the chilling effect into analysis on the margin means asking whether the incremental benefit of encouraging the expression of some truths, which is hypothetical and certainly unobservable, is proportionate to the concrete and measurable harm in the case at hand. With respect to the former we may be able to make reasonably confident though only intuitive judgments about largish categories of expression even if we are unable to do so in the incremental manner required by proportionality. This may provide another argument against a too finely grained structure of free expression doctrine.

2.3   Indirect arguments more generally

Direct arguments for and against regulation invoke underlying political theories of free expression. They are often unsuitable because of reasonable dispute over both what underlying political theory is best and what the chosen political theory implies. Institutional arguments like that generating the 'chilling effect' idea operate at a different level. They are second-order arguments applicable no matter what one's preferred political theory of free expression is, because they direct attention – in this example – to the specific institutional ways in which expression is disseminated and its permissibility determined. We have seen several second-order arguments already, and the idea of second-order arguments can be fleshed out with other examples.

In an important early statement, the US Supreme Court wrote:

> There are certain well-defined and narrowly limited classes of speech, the prevention and punishment of which have never been thought to raise any Constitutional problem . . . It has been well observed that such utterances

are no essential part of any exposition of ideas, and are of such slight social value as a step to truth that any benefit that may be derived from them is clearly outweighed by the social interest in order and morality.[2]

This statement has two themes, a historical one ('never been thought') and a functional one ('slight social value . . . outweighed by the social interest'). When it considered the statute banning 'crush porn' (Chapter 1.4), the Supreme Court rejected the functional test in favor of the historical one, describing the former as 'dangerous' because it was 'highly manipulable'. The concern here cannot be that the Supreme Court would itself manipulate the functional test, because whenever the Court applied the test it would necessarily not think that it was manipulating the test in any pejorative sense. Rather, the concern is that legislatures and lower courts would do so and the Supreme Court would be unable effectively to review every such manipulation – again, an institutional argument.

The US Supreme Court offered a similar second-order argument when it held the Stolen Valor Act unconstitutional because it was not aimed at any fairly identifiable material harm (Chapter 1.4). The requirement of material harm provided a 'limiting principle' that could effectively constrain the government from 'compil[ing] a list of subjects about which false statements are punishable'. Justice Stephen Breyer invoked the chilling effect idea in support for that conclusion.

The second-order argument here might be plausible if the question was whether a legislature could enact a general statute making it unlawful to disseminate false statements of whatever sort even if they did not cause material harm. It is perhaps less plausible in connection with statutes identifying *specific* false statements, such as Holocaust denial. One important institutional difference between libel law and a Holocaust denial statute is precisely that the former is general, with individual plaintiffs able to initiate lawsuits, whereas the latter is specific. In light of constraints on legislative time, legislatures will not enact many such specific statutes, as experience around the world shows. Justice Breyer worried that allowing legislatures to impose liability for false statements that do not cause material harm would allow them to enact statutes prohibiting 'little white lies', as they are known, that can, for example 'provide the sick with comfort'. That worry seems overstated. Higher

---

2 Chaplinsky v. United States 315 U.S. 568 (1942). Among the materials not covered by free expression, as developed in Chapter 3, were the obscene, the libelous, and fighting words.

courts should have no difficulty in determining whether the small hand-ful of false statements (that do not cause material harm) legislatures single out for attention strike a reasonable balance between social value, assumed to be small or zero in the case of falsity, and public interests.

The same can be said about the perhaps more troublesome problem of controversy over whether statements singled out for legislative attention are factually false. One can just barely imagine legislatures in the United States enacting statutes premised on the idea that assertions that climate change has human causes are factually false, or that so-called creation science is false. We could allow liability to be imposed when a person makes a false factual assertion about climate change knowing that asser-tion to be false – that is, for lying. This would distinguish between the Stolen Valor Act, which could readily have been interpreted to require such a showing, and Holocaust denial, which is typically promulgated by people who believe that what they are saying is true.

Proponents of Holocaust denial laws, though, would not find that approach satisfying, precisely because most Holocaust deniers are not lying in that sense. An alternative approach would be to allow liability for disseminating demonstrably false statements of fact, where the demonstration is made in the first instance by a legislature enact-ing a specific statute, and then by a decision-maker determining that someone has indeed made such a false statement. How do institutional arguments work here? At the first stage the question is whether we must be concerned with distorted legislative judgments. Sometimes it is said, and sometimes accurately, that statutes aimed at penalizing the dissemination of specific lies result from 'political correctness'. The point is driven home by pointing to quite similar falsehoods that are left unpunished. So, for example, a legislature might punish Holocaust denial but not denials that the treatment of Armenians in Turkey in the 1910s was genocide, explained – in this setting – by the fact that Turks and their domestic supporters have more political power than Armenians and theirs, compared to the opponents and proponents of Holocaust denial. Even if the 'political correctness' claim is true, it might well be irrelevant, being simply an example of how pluralist politics works: As noted earlier, the mere fact that speech-infringing legislation is 'special interest' legislation will rarely weigh heavily against its permissibility.

Next we should ask whether we have the institutional capacity to determine whether the legislature has singled out a category of statements that are reasonably thought to be demonstrably false. That is the determination at stake in the contrast between Holocaust denial statutes and the hypothetical climate change statute. Even if we thought that courts did have that capacity, there still might be questions at the second stage. At that stage a decision-maker – a jury, in the United States, a judge elsewhere – has to decide whether, for example, the assertion that 'only' three million people were killed by Nazis is Holocaust denial. We might be skeptical about decision-makers' ability to decide that question appropriately, that is, in a way that leaves room for reasonable disagreements about precisely what the scope of the Nazi extermination program was.

A final problem might arise if lies, while not intrinsically valuable, have socially valuable consequences. The most prominent examples – and perhaps the only ones – are what might be called 'journalistic lies'. These are deceptive statements made by investigative journalists to gain access to material that would not be made available were the possessors to know that the person seeking it was a journalist. So, for example, a journalist may pose as a job-seeker to gain access to places where animals are killed for food, misrepresenting her prior experience and perhaps even expressly denying that she is a journalist. With access to the slaughterhouse, the journalist will be in a position to write stories about the sanitary conditions there, stories that will inform public discussion about matters ranging from food safety to vegetarianism.

How should we think about this problem? First, we should distinguish two possibilities. In the first, liability is imposed on the journalist for résumé fraud, a statute of 'general applicability', to use a term that we will see again. Here our first question should be one of statutory interpretation: Should the general résumé fraud statute be interpreted to apply to journalistic lies of this sort? If it is so interpreted, we would ask whether the general statute minimally impairs free expression, or is the least restrictive means of avoiding the obvious social harms associated with résumé fraud. At this point we return to the general questions noted earlier about those tests.

The second possibility involves a statute aimed specifically at journalistic lies. Some jurisdictions within the United States have adopted such statutes, and they are clearly the product of special interest lobbying by the agriculture industry, though they might sometimes be promoted by other industries. Yet, it might be difficult to show that the special interest influence produced a misestimation of social costs and benefits. Most obviously, there are special interests on both sides here – the agriculture industry on one side, and the institutional press, with its interest in investigative journalism, on the other. Agricultural interests say, with some support, that many investigations generate stories that attract wide public attention but that are misleading even if technically true; the institutional press says, also with some support, that most investigations produced as a result of journalistic lies provide important information relevant to many matters of public concern. On the face of things, it is unclear that the possibility of legislative misestimation is any greater with respect to statutes aimed at journalistic lies than with respect to any other type of special interest legislation.

The final step would be to ask whether there is a risk of distorted judgment at the implementation stage even if the legislature's estimates are not obviously distorted. Here institutional concerns come to the fore. Who exactly will be implementing the statute? We might imagine that a statute authorizing a 'department of agriculture' to impose liability on journalists would be implemented with a thumb on the scales favoring the agriculture industry. In the United States, we might worry about the possibility that lawsuits against journalists would be decided by juries drawn from areas in which agriculture was a far more important local interest than journalism. Thinking about these institutional details and their implications for implementation might be more productive than thinking about the level of legislative decision.

To return to the beginning: One might hold the political theory that free expression is important primarily or even only because it is the best means we have for determining truth. Within such a theory, falsity about facts has no more than minimal value, if it has any at all. Yet, even within that theory institutional or second-order arguments are available to support the rather strong intuitions that many people have that free expression law should place some limits on the government's ability to punish people for making false factual assertions.

Second-order arguments allow us to finesse disputes about what underlying political theory is best. Such arguments of course rest on claims about institutional capacity and the like, and those claims are contestable, particularly on the margins. But, in focusing on institutions, they operate within a domain far more familiar to lawyers than is political theory, and for that reason may support free expression law more robustly than direct or first-order arguments do.

The US Supreme Court's preference for the historical over the functional analysis illustrates another second- or perhaps third-order argument – the use of a preferred theory of constitutional interpretation (sometimes referred to in the United States as a 'constitutional theory'). Again, there are direct arguments for theories of interpretation. A historical approach, or 'originalism', is said to respect agreements made at the constitution's founding that have normative weight over time and to constrain judges better than alternatives; a 'living constitution' approach is said to accommodate founding commitments with contemporary preferences and evolving understandings of a nation's basic commitments. And, as with direct arguments for free expression based on political theory, direct arguments for theories of constitutional interpretation typically founder on the shoals of reasonable disagreement.

There may be, though, indirect arguments for the choice of a constitutional theory. These arguments take a now-familiar form. Consider originalism: Its proponents argue that its focus on historical understandings limits the information that must be considered by those deliberating about constitutional questions. An inquiry limited in that way is, they say, likely to produce better results, overall, than a 'living constitution' approach that licenses decision-makers to consider contemporary mores (which, proponents of originalism say, means consulting their own intuitions), social-science evidence about the consequences of one or another interpretation, and much more. Of course, proponents should concede, sometimes a purely historical inquiry will misfire, with decision-makers interpreting the historical materials in light of their contemporary presuppositions and inclinations. And sometimes a completely honest historical inquiry will generate results inconsistent with contemporary values. But, the second-order argument goes, the simplified historical inquiry, conducted by decision-makers with limited time, knowledge, and intellectual capacity, will generate enough correct results to outweigh the inevitable unreviewable errors.

As with all second-order arguments, this one rests on disputable claims about institutional characteristics and capacities. Some of those claims are particularly vulnerable to criticism. The relevant decision-makers are lawyers and legislators, not historians, for example, and they might be much better at discerning contemporary values, as living constitutionalism counsels, than at understanding the historical materials. More generally, the claims about institutional capacity associated with second-order theories of constitutional interpretation seem far more diffuse and difficult to verify than those associated with the more specific institutional accounts already sketched. That said, thinking about choices among theories of constitutional interpretation at a second-order problem might end up being more productive than attempting to reach agreement on direct accounts of constitutional interpretation.

3 The distinction between coverage and protection

3.1 Introduction

A person wants to open a grocery store that will sell only locally sourced food, but chooses a location zoned for residential not commercial activities. Can she even get a claim off the ground that the zoning regulation adversely affects (infringes) her right to freedom of expression? Suppose she says that operating such a store is her way of communicating to the public her view that consuming locally sourced food is the best way to combat the pernicious political influence of Big Agriculture, and augments that assertion by pointing out that she is very good at running stores but quite bad at articulating in words the beliefs that she wants to communicate.

Most people react to this example by denying that the freedom of expression is even relevant to the analysis. In Professor Frederick Schauer's evocative phrase, freedom of expression does not even show up when we think about the grocer's problem. Some constitutional systems have provisions clearly more suitable to address it: the right to choose one's occupation or the right to free development of the personality, for example. The grocer's claim might bring those constitutional provisions into play, but not the freedom of expression. The analytic point is that the freedom of expression's domain is limited. In the helpful term used in US law, the freedom of expression has limited *coverage*.

Limits on the freedom of expression's coverage arise as well from specific constitutional language. The US Constitution refers to 'the freedom of speech'. All agree that this provision covers at least some forms of non-verbal expression, but which ones, and why? The German Basic Law provides: 'Every person shall have the right freely to express and disseminate his opinions is speech, writing, and pictures . . .' The International Covenant on Civil and Political Rights provides: 'Everyone shall have the right to freedom of expression; this right shall include freedom to seek, receive and impart information and ideas of all kinds, . . . either orally, in writing or in print, in the form of art, or through any other media of his choice.'

Not all communication involves opinions or ideas, though. Noticing this, the Basic Law's drafters included a separate provision: 'Art and scholarship, research, and teaching shall be free.' This reshapes but does not eliminate the question of coverage. Is the freedom to express opinions in speech 'stronger' than the freedom of art? If so, it will matter whether some activity is speech expressing an opinion or is instead artistic expression. And if they are equally strong, what is the point of distinguishing them? It would not have been difficult to draft the freedom of expression provisions without referring to 'opinions' or 'ideas'.

The language of strength suggests why one cannot completely finesse the question of coverage by invoking proportionality, that is, by saying that, no matter what the coverage of these provisions, every infringe-ment on the interests protected by each provision must be justified as proportionate. That response might make the elaboration of specific rights legally unnecessary. A complete bill of rights could consist of a single sentence: 'Every infringement on a human interest must be justified as proportionate.' We might want a highly elaborated bill of rights for other reasons, of course – as a way of communicating to a lay public the idea that the government's power is limited, for example. Identifying specific rights, though, would be unimportant for legal purposes.

That seems inconsistent with the language of constitutional docu-ments. What would German constitutional law make of a verbal threat of physical violence uttered at the outset of a brawl in a bar? It would be difficult to contend that the threat is an expression of an opinion without leaching the term 'opinion' of real content, nor is the threat artistic. A restriction on the ability to make such threats might be described as an interference with the right to free development of the personality. That possibility, though, shows that the question of cover-age arises even under proportionality analysis.

Alexy's terms, high and low, might provide some help here. The idea is that some rights are generically high, meaning that infringements of them require stronger justifications than infringements of other inter-ests such as, perhaps, the right to free development of the personality.

Importantly, as noted in Chapter 1, this introduces a degree of categorical analysis into proportionality: Classifying something as speech expressing an opinion or an idea triggers a requirement of strong justification; classifying it as art means that a sufficient justification might be a weaker one.[1]

Having made free expression law somewhat categorical, we might ask: Why not go further, as US law does – and as nearly every jurist who provides examples of proportionality analysis does? The US law of free expression expressly distinguishes types of speech based on the value of its content, in a categorical way: Some speech, prototypically speech about public policy, is generically of high value, some, prototypically commercial advertising, has intermediate value, and some speech, such as sexually explicit but non-obscene speech, has low value. And, as noted, some verbal expressions are simply outside the coverage of freedom of expression. Proportionality analysts typically use similar concepts, though often in a case-specific way or, as suggested in Chapter 1, using more categories than US law does.

Consider two cases involving explicit verbal and photographic depictions of sexual activity. One involves material that simply presents those depictions one after another, the other presents a story line parodying some recent political events. Under US law, the question will be whether the material is obscene. Given the definition of obscenity, both might be obscene, in which case both fall outside the coverage of freedom of expression. Those using proportionality might conclude, in contrast, that the first case involves material that can be suppressed if suppression is supported by a rather weak justification, whereas the justification for suppressing the second might have to be somewhat stronger.

These examples introduce the distinction between coverage and protection. Regulated material is covered by the freedom of expression if the distinctive modes of justification associated with freedom of expression are triggered. Material is protected if the regulation is unjustified. Under US law, obscene materials are not covered by freedom of expression, other sexually explicit materials are – and receive 'full' protection subject to some qualifications discussed below. Under

---

1 This is not a claim that German constitutional law actually treats opinions in speech differently from art, but rather an effort to lay bare the proposition that every enumeration of specific rights necessarily leads to questions about each right's coverage.

proportionality, all sexually explicitly materials are covered by freedom of expression and art, but some receive weaker protection than others, that is, can be regulated with weaker justifications.

We turn to two areas in which the distinction between coverage and protection arises: the protection afforded non-verbal artistic expression such as dance and non-representational art, and the protection afforded commercial advertising. The distinction is analytically interesting but inconsequential in the first area, because almost everyone agrees that non-verbal artistic expression is protected to the same degree as verbal expressions (whatever the degree of protection is). In contrast, the distinction is consequential in connection with commercial advertising.

3.2 Artistic and other forms of non-verbal expression

Totalitarian governments not infrequently attempt to control artistic expression – the Soviet promotion of 'socialist realism', the Nazi attack on 'degenerate art', for example. Reasonably democratic governments rarely do so directly. Sometimes they make regulatory judgments about zoning that incorporate esthetic judgments about what sorts of artistic displays would be suitable for residential areas. More often, they subsidize the production and display of art that conforms to esthetic and popular criteria. These regulations tend to be relatively mild compared to suppression: An art work that cannot be displayed in one venue can ordinarily be displayed in another; an artist who fails to receive a government grant might be able to find a private patron.[2]

Non-verbal actions that clearly communicate *some* messages do not always convey clear ones. Around the world controversies have arisen about the constitutionality of prohibiting burning of the national flag. Flag-burning surely conveys a general message of disdain for and opposition to the government in power, but in itself does not identify what it is about the government that deserves criticism. Still, it seems unquestionable that non-verbal activity that conveys an understandable message is covered by freedom of expression. The formulation in US law is helpful: Non-verbal activities are covered if they are intended to communicate something and are likely to do so.

---

2 For an overview of the issues associated with non-verbal expression, see Mark Tushnet, Joseph Blocher, and Alan Chen, Free Speech beyond Words: The Surprising Reach of the First Amendment (New York: New York University Press, 2017).

Yet, focusing on the meaning of artistic and non-verbal expression – what the expression communicates – can misfire. What a work of art means is often contested. Even more, some artists and scholars contend that art does not 'mean' anything. For them it does not 'impart information or ideas' or 'express an opinion'. This, or at least something like it, is almost certainly true of modern non-representational art and modern artistic dance, which are often the artist's attempts to explore shapes, space, form, and movement.

Even so, few scholars of freedom of expression doubt that artistic expression is covered. Briefly examining the reasons offered for that conclusion produces an important result: There may be no necessary and sufficient conditions for determining whether some human activity is covered by freedom of expression; rather, covered activities have a family resemblance. To return to the grocery store owner: Her activity is not covered by freedom of expression, but not because it lacks characteristics necessary to qualify for coverage and even if it has some characteristics in common with activities that *are* covered.

Artistic endeavors are clearly connected to the autonomy-related accounts of free expression. Indeed, the romantic image of the artist struggling to find the means of expressing herself in her art is important in many cultures. Yet there is nothing especially distinctive about the connection between autonomy and art. The grocer who wants to promote locally sourced foods is also expressing her autonomy.

The connection between artistic endeavors and the pursuit and discovery of truth is more obscure. Truth-related accounts are often summarized with reference to the marketplace of ideas, and that metaphor suggests the difficulty in the present context. The market test of truth with respect to art is obscure largely because the forms of interest for art are not about – do not convey – ideas. They may induce people to think, or to reflect on the physical world, or appreciate the capacity of humans to create beauty, but those mental processes are at most loosely connected to the discovery of truth. Perhaps through those processes viewing art improves our ability to evaluate factual claims and political positions. On this account, viewing art is something like a form of mental gymnastics, an exercise without any special point of its own, but that strengthens our cognitive abilities. Here too art does not seem particularly distinctive: Taking hikes in the woods, working in the fields, simply meditating – all these might have effects similar to those sketched here. Regulations infringing these activities might be analyzed under the heading of the right to free development of the personality, and so too might regulations adversely affecting the interest in producing artistic works.

Alexander Meiklejohn, the US theorist of free expression, made a similar argument about the connection between art and democratic self-government. Self-government, Meiklejohn wrote, 'can exist only insofar as voters acquire . . . intelligence, integrity, sensitivity, and generous devotion to the general welfare', and 'literature and the arts' are among the 'forms of thought and expression' assisting voters in acquiring those abilities.[3] True enough, but so do many other activities not covered by freedom of expression, with our grocer serving once again as the example. Professor Robert Bork offered sexual activities as another example. Those activities might be covered by some constitutional protections, such as the right to free development of the personality, but, Bork argued, they were not covered by freedom of expression even though participating in them helped people acquire intelligence, integrity, and sensitivity.

Bork differed from most scholars in the field in concluding that art was not covered by free expression. Yet, none of the discrete theories of free expression are fully adequate to support the consensus. Rather, art and other non-verbal activities are covered by free expression (when they are) because they are sufficiently similar to material that is unquestionably covered. The similarity is, in terms drawn from the philosophy of language, a family resemblance. And, on one account of family resemblances of that type, we know that matters share a family resemblance because we participate in a community of discourse, whose understandings, importantly, can change. It may be, then, that identifying matters covered by freedom of expression may require the exercise of a culturally and temporally specific form of legal judgment. Specifically, what is covered by freedom of expression may differ from one legal culture to another, and even within a single legal culture from one time to another.

3.3 Commercial advertising

The distinction between coverage and protection can be explored further by considering the regulation of commercial advertising.

---

3 Alexander Meiklejohn, 'Free Speech Is an Absolute', 1961 Supreme Court Review 245 (1961).

Suppose our free expression law followed what can be called an 'outside-inside' model. In that model, everything not covered by free expression receives no protection as expression (though it may receive protection under some other constitutional provisions), and everything covered by free expression is fully and equally protected. The lesson drawn around the world from experience with sedition law (Chapter 1.5) is that speech critical of government policy can be regulated only if quite strict standards are met. Setting aside specific doctrinal formulations and concerns that shape sedition law itself, we can say that full protection means that regulation is permissible only when it serves a compelling (extremely important) public interest, and does so in a way that limits regulation to expression that has a close causal connection to the harm the government seeks to avert (an idea captured in most formulations as a requirement that the regulation be narrowly tailored to its goals, or that it be the least restrictive alternative for doing so).

Strict tests are manifestly unsuitable for many matters covered by free expression that governments permissibly regulate. Commercial advertising provides a good example. Often governments regulate advertising to ensure that consumers are not misled, or to discourage what the legislature reasonably believes to be socially undesirable behavior (though not so undesirable as to justify a complete prohibition). Regulations may prescribe the conditions under which a product can be advertised as 'low calorie' or 'lite', so that consumers who wish to buy only low-calorie foods will be able to fulfil their desires. Regulations may limit the forms and venues for advertising tobacco products to discourage young people from acquiring a taste for tobacco. The public purposes underlying these regulations are undoubtedly important, but we can fairly wonder whether they are as important – as compelling – as the interest in reducing the risk that constitutionally valid laws will be violated. Nor (often) are there reasons to think that the legislature's judgment on the relevant matters is distorted by self-interest and the like. And, at least as important, we can quite often wonder whether the regulations will actually achieve their goals, or achieve them well enough to satisfy a strict requirement of causal connection. Will consumers actually understand that a 'lite' label means only that the product has no more than half the calories of an unlabeled product, rather than having almost no calories? Indeed, how many consumers will even notice the 'lite' label when they compare prices for products?

Full and equal protection for everything covered by free expression might produce undesirable results. Seeking to give legislatures leeway to regulate commercial advertising, we would develop a standard that would allow them to regulate too much political speech. Or, more importantly, seeking adequately to protect political speech, we would be forced to apply a strict standard and invalidate many seemingly valuable regulations of commercial advertising. Perhaps decision-makers could resist these competing pressures, and in particular might accept protecting 'too much' commercial advertising as a cost worth bearing for protecting political speech adequately. It might be better, though, to develop a doctrinal structure that would not generate those pressures.

As before, here too we confront the question of how finely grained the structure should be. The 'outside-inside' model uses the largest categories available. Proportionality analysis understood as an approach that is rather finely grained (though not entirely case-specific) uses much smaller categories. We can call this the 'onion' model. Deep inside the 'onion' lies political speech, which receives the highest degree of protection. The core is surrounded by layer after layer of different types of speech, each receiving slightly less protection than its more inward neighbor but slightly more than its outward one. These varying degrees of protection could be formulated as numerous different tests for constitutionality, or folded into a more general proportionality test. When we reach the limit of coverage, material just inside free expression's coverage receives a bit more protection than material outside it – that is, its regulation is tested against a standard only a bit tougher than the test applied to material outside free expression's coverage. (There are hints of the onion model even in US constitutional law, the prime example being the zoning regulation of adult bookstores discussed in Chapter 1.4.)

A key question about the onion model is how thick the layers are (another way of asking how finely grained the analysis will be). The onion model generates its own pressures, which may be as troublesome as the pressures that arise in connection with the 'outside-inside' model. Consider yet again the 'indirect encouragement of terrorism' statute. Such encouragement is neither an argument for committing terroristic acts, nor incitement to commit them. Using the onion model, a decision-maker could conclude that indirect encouragement of terrorism is one thin layer removed from the core of political speech, still quite strongly protected but not quite as protected as core political speech – indeed, just enough less protected to make the regulation constitutionally permissible. In the onion model, that is, there will be pressure to proliferate layers in a not quite ad hoc way, so as to allow regulation of material just slightly different from similar material that does receive protection.

Again, there is a hint of this process in US constitutional law. The US Supreme Court upheld a statute punishing giving material support to terrorist organizations by means of instruction, coordinated with the groups, about international human rights and methods of peaceful dispute resolution available in international forums.[4] As the Court explained the result, such instruction would unquestionably be fully protected without the coordination and connection to terrorist groups. But, it held, the statute survived the strict inquiry required at the core of free expression. Nominally, the Court adhered to the 'outside-inside' model, but the result seems easier to explain through the onion model.

There is one obvious way to reduce the pressure to proliferate layers in the onion model: use relatively thick layers – or, to revert to the more general term, make the doctrine only moderately finely grained. Questions and pressures will, of course, arise at the boundaries between the layers, but because there are fewer of them, the pressures may be easier to resist and even if the decision-maker succumbs to the pressure the occasions for doing so will be fewer.

Another admittedly more strained vegetable metaphor captures a version of this alternative that may better describe US doctrine: Rather than an onion, think of an avocado, with an extremely hard core surrounded by pulpy flesh. The core consists of high-value speech – political, literary, and artistic, to use some conventional labels – and the flesh consists of everything else. The test of constitutionality for high-value speech is a quite stringent one, while the test for everything else is a balancing test that is sensitive to many considerations, including the type of speech being regulated.

As noted earlier, the US law of free expression is usually described as employing three categories, with commercial advertising and perhaps some other materials receiving greater protection than sexually explicit but non-obscene speech, but not as much protection as political and many other materials. The precise number of categories is less important, though, than the conclusion that it might be helpful to have a smallish number of categories rather than, as the rhetoric

---

4 Holder v. Humanitarian Law Project, 561 U.S. 1 (2010).

of proportionality tends to suggest, a relatively large number of them. This repeats the conclusion of the argument outlined in Chapter 1.4.

3.4   What lies at the core? A listener-focused approach

The onion model isolates some forms of speech at the core, though of course such speech is covered and typically protected in all models. The core consists of political speech, defined both as speech supporting or opposing political candidates and as speech supporting, opposing, or describing public policies whether those policies are currently a subject of political contention or merely proposed for future adoption. Any sensible free expression law will give substantial protection to political speech.

Should that protection vary depending on the reasons the speaker has for engaging in political speech? Motivations can vary: a person might criticize a candidate because she believes that the candidate's election would be bad for the public; a corporation might publish advertisements supporting a proposal because its enactment would increase the corporation's profits; or a person might criticize a candidate out of personal animus or to get revenge for some personal slight, real or imagined. If one thought motivation mattered, the varying motivations might affect how proportionality analysis would be applied, or affect whether the regulation is treated as inside the core or as a different layer in the onion model. Administering a motivation-oriented rule might be quite difficult, but one can imagine a system that imposed limits on corporate expenditures on advertising dealing with politics – even advertising purporting to describe why some proposal would advance the public good.

Yet, relatively few accounts of free expression law treat motivation as relevant to legal analysis. Consider a speaker who discloses some past misconduct by a political candidate merely to get back at that candidate, without regard to whether he believes that that misconduct has any bearing on the candidate's fitness to serve. Most accounts hold that it would be inconsistent with principles of free expression to regulate badly motivated disclosures, wholly apart from difficulties of administering any such regulation. The reason is obvious: Whether or not the speaker believes that the disclosure has some bearing on the candidate's fitness to serve, others might believe that it does, and the disclosure enhances their ability to assess the candidate's fitness.

This argument, while clearly appealing, introduces an important shift in the focus of free expression law, from the speaker's interest to the interests of listeners. A listener-focused account of free expression has quite broad implications, many of which differ from those flowing from speaker-focused accounts.

3.4.1 Listener focus as a systemic account

Philosopher Alexander Meiklejohn drew upon the image of a town meeting to explain why a listener-focused account made sense. The time available for a town meeting is limited, and some rules are required to ensure that discussion of policy proposals is as productive as it can be. For Meiklejohn, those rules might include restrictions on speakers: 'What is essential is not that everyone shall speak, but that everything worth saying shall be said.'[5] On this view, those running the meeting can ask of someone who seeks to speak: 'Do you have anything to say on this proposal that's different from what's been said already?' and can deny the opportunity to speak if the answer is 'No' so that another opinion – something else 'worth saying' – can be expressed. The Constitutional Council in France offered a similar view in dealing with a law on press concentration. It said that free expression required that the public 'have a sufficient number of publications [available] of different trends and characters'.[6]

The governing idea here is that the system of free expression should provide listeners with all the information they need to participate in political decision-making. The presence of the words 'worth saying' and 'sufficient number' in the formulations of the listener-focused account is a signal that once again we have to use the basic idea, about deference to reasonable legislative choices. On the listener-focused account, the question to ask is not whether a particular speaker is unable to say what she wants, but rather whether the set of regulations (including the one that limits this particular speaker), taken as a whole, creates a system that does a reasonable job of ensuring public participation in policy-making – or, again more precisely, whether legislators could reasonably believe that the set of regulations does so.

---

5 Alexander Meiklejohn, Free Speech and its Relation to Self-Government (Clark, NJ: The Lawbook Exchange Ltd., 1948).

6 Constitutional Council, Decision 84–181 on press concentration.

Meiklejohn used the town meeting metaphor as a convenient way of getting across the idea of a listener-focused account. The metaphor involves a situation in which time was necessarily limited. One might think that the account would be irrelevant when there were no similar limits, as in the press concentration case: Nothing stands in the way of producing and distributing as many copies of as many newspapers as there might be. Yet, Meiklejohn's metaphor was merely an expository device, not intrinsic to the account. And, if one wanted, one could extend the metaphor: Even outside the context of a town meeting, people have limited time and energy to devote to politics. To use the press concentration example: Suppose the vast majority of media outlets – newspapers and radio and television stations – are owned by a single entity. Legislators might (reasonably?) believe that that entity would flood the society with a single message, thereby drowning out – in the metaphor usually employed – other things 'worth saying', other 'trends and characters'. Extending the metaphor, though, is unnecessary. A listener-focused account, dealing with the system of regulations as a whole, is an alternative to speaker-focused accounts, defensible as a reasonable choice among available political-theory accounts of free expression (and democracy). The listener-focused account, that is, is community and society oriented rather than individually focused.

That a listener-focused account deals with the system of free expression – the set of rules rather than any individual rule – has major ramifications. Rules that would be quite vulnerable under many speaker-focused accounts might be easily defensible under a listener-focused account: If what this particular speaker wants to say will be said by someone else, barring her from saying it would be permissible. And, indeed, were we to examine regulation of political speech in reasonably well-functioning democracies, we would be hard-pressed to find a set of rules that makes it impossible to say something 'worth saying'.[7] Generally, it seems quite unlikely that a legislature in such a democracy would adopt a set of rules inconsistent with a reasonable listener-focused account of free expression.

---

7 Note that one cannot counter this proposition by pointing to policy positions, such as indirect advocacy of terrorism, that are permissibly banned under a speaker-focused account of free expression. One would have to identify policy positions that are protected under a speaker-focused approach but would be permissibly regulated under a listener-focused one.

3.4.2   Listener focus and the problem of regulating political campaigns

Constitutional democracies around the world have struggled with the problem of financing political campaigns. The role of money in elections threatens to produce corruption in several senses: the personal enrichment of candidates through selling their votes, once elected, to donors; the distortion of public policy when contracts are awarded to bidders who contributed to campaigns, or when policies are adopted with more attention to the interests of donors than to the public interest; and more. Yet, restricting contributions and, even more, expenditures raises questions about free expression. And, often, the basic idea of deference to reasonable legislative choices seems to be offset by the possibility that legislative judgment is distorted by precisely legislators' interests in adopting systems of campaign finance regulation that benefit themselves either directly, by allowing contributions that amount to bribes, or indirectly, by making it easier for them to defend their seats against challengers. Speaker-focused analyses of campaign finance regulations lead to the conclusion that many forms of regulation are inconsistent with free expression. Listener-focused analyses might be more promising, but they might lead to the ratification of regulatory systems that entrench incumbents.

Two points should be made at the outset. First, it is sometimes said that regulations of campaign finance raise no distinctive problems of free expression because money is not speech. That is too facile, as essentially all courts and scholars who have addressed the issue have agreed. The reason is that money, while not speech itself, is a prerequisite to speech. Even the single speaker who expresses her view at a town meeting might have to spend money to buy a bus ticket to get to the meeting. And, more seriously, many people with strong policy views or views about candidates are not especially articulate in explaining their positions, and even if they can do so, they might find it difficult to disseminate their views without assistance. Such people can hire others to give their views coherence and power (speech writers, advertising executives), and can spend money on the resources to spread their views by printing pamphlets, recording advertisements to be broadcast on radio and television or social media, and buying time and space in the media to place those advertisements. It is plainly unreasonable to contend that regulation of those activities, all of which are 'merely' financial, has nothing to do with free expression. As we will see, perhaps the best way to address the role of money in politics is through doctrines dealing with content-neutral regulations of expression (Chapter 5), but that regulation of campaign finance is regulation of expression seems indisputable.

At the same time an important intuition may be at work here, that some *forms* of electioneering should be relatively insensitive to wealth. Suppose, for example, debates among candidates became an important feature of some elections, and those debates were sponsored by private organizations. We might be concerned about a government-imposed rule identifying who the organizations must allow into the debates, but not about a similar regulation barring participants from bidding for the amount of screen time they can have. The reason is that candidate debates have an identifiable social function as to which wealth should be irrelevant. Perhaps other features of political campaigns have this characteristic as well – though contributions and expenditures, the core concern in the area, almost certainly do not.

Second, many proponents of campaign finance regulation believe that such regulations can promote an interest independent of avoiding corruption – the interest in fair political competition, often described as having a level playing field. The thought is that grossly unequal expenditures by parties or candidates tilt the playing field in favor of the big spenders, who gain an undeserved advantage. Spelling out why the advantage is undeserved, or more generally what it means to have a level playing field, is quite difficult. Some candidates will have few financial resources because few people support them; the fact that they are outspent by more popular candidates says nothing about whether the playing field is level or tilted.

The most sensible version of the interest in fair political competition is that parties and candidates should have resources roughly in proportion to their support. This version might have some purchase in nations with two or three large parties and a handful of reasonably permanent minor parties. Even there, one will encounter problems. Consider a party that won the most recent election by 53 percent to 47 percent, but that has lost popularity because it adopted policies now regarded by many as disastrous. It is hardly obvious that that party would have 53 or even 50 percent of the resources on a level playing field. Nor is it obvious, though, that on a level playing field the opposition party would have the resources measured by current support in (inevitably inaccurate) opinion polls.

The problem of determining when the playing field is level is even more serious in systems in which parties bubble up around a specific leader, flourish for one or two elections, and then subside. What is a level playing field on which an outsider challenges the existing parties root and branch? Even legislators seeking to advance the public good would have difficulty figuring out how to develop systems of regulating campaign finance that work well when a Green Party – much less a Pirate Party (which clearly seemed a joke when initially formed, and then became a serious minor party in several nations) – comes on the scene. The problem of distorted legislative judgment arises rather dramatically here: Legislators will typically want to make it difficult for these parties to get a foothold in the electoral system.

These difficulties suggest that the interest in promoting fair terms of political competition should play a distinctly secondary role in free expression law's application to campaign finance regulation.

With that background, we can turn to the heart of the topic. Systems of campaign finance regulation deal with a wide range of topics. These include regulation of expenditures by candidates and parties, regulation of contributions to candidates and parties, and public financing of campaigns. By considering just one of the topics within the field – regulation of spending by individuals (or corporations) to express their support of candidates and policies, where that spending is not coordinated with spending by candidates or parties (known in the United States as independent expenditures) – we can compare speaker-focused approaches with listener-focused ones. To preview the conclusion: A listener-focused approach provides a more direct route than a speaker-focused one to results that many appear to believe normatively attractive.

The US Supreme Court and the European Court of Human Rights have held that low limits on expenditures violate principles of free expression.[8] Anyone who wants to express her support for or opposition to a candidate or policy has to spend something if she is to get her views across to those outside her circle of friends. Suppose, though, that she cares deeply about the candidate or issue, and wants to spend everything she has to get her message across as widely and effectively as she can, up to her personally set limit on spending. The amount she

---

8 Randall v. Sorrell, 548 U.S. 230 (2006) (involving spending limits for candidates); Bowman v. United Kingdom, [1998] ECtHR 4.

spends is a rough measure of the intensity of her concern (as limited by her personal financial resources). Denying her the ability to spend whatever she chooses seems a substantial limitation on her right of free expression, taking into account the combination of intensity and personal resources. This is a speaker-focused approach to the problem.

What justification might there be for such a limitation? Consider first spending that takes a position on an issue – pro-choice or anti-abortion, for example. It is unclear that a government has *any* interest in restricting issue-spending. Perhaps it is that massive spending on one side of an issue is incompatible with fair political competition. But, as noted above, it is quite difficult to come up with a defensible account of fair political competition. In the context of issue-advocacy, for example, the intensity of views for and against the policy is relevant to determining whether the competition is fair, and spending is a proxy – imperfect, as all proxies are – for intensity.

Additional problems might arise if the issue is associated with political candidates, or in connection with spending on advocacy about candidates. The concern is that such spending might lead to corruption. A successful candidate might do favors for her supporters unrelated to the issues that led them to support her. Or, perhaps more serious, candidates might use false-fronts to evade limitations on *candidate* expenditures: Behind the scenes of nominally independent spending, the candidate is actually dictating the spending. Limiting independent spending might be a way to police the limits on candidate spending. Indeed, it might be the least restrictive way of doing so; allowing someone to spend above the prescribed limits if she establishes that the spending is truly independent of the candidate might be administratively difficult, and a sensible allocation of public resources to investigate such claims might lead to a higher level of evasion than is desirable.

Note the presence of words like 'might' throughout this argument. Courts taking a speaker-focused approach must decide how much weight to give to possibilities and risks – or, again more precisely, must decide how much weight to give to a decision by a (possibly biased) legislature about possibilities and risks. Assume that the court takes the most aggressive stance possible: Skeptical about the legislature's ability to make reasonable judgments about possibilities and risks, the court makes its own evaluation of them. We might wonder about the availability of distinctively legal criteria for doing so, and as a result wonder about whether the court will simply make a rough-and-ready judgment that the regulations are 'too strict' or 'not too strict'. At least within a speaker-focused framework, we might be forced to choose which is the lesser of two evils – an analysis that gives substantial leeway to a possibly biased legislature, or one that authorizes courts to make quite discretionary judgments about how much regulation is too much.

There is an alternative, of course: hold that all limitations on spending are inconsistent with free expression. Yet, even in the United States, where the constitutional protection given to political speech is perhaps the greatest in the world, that remains a minority position. Decisions finding that restrictions do not allow 'enough' spending implicitly – and sometimes explicitly – reject the proposition that spending limits are impermissible: Saying that a specific limit is too low suggests that some limit would be 'high enough', though of course without specifying how high the limit would have to be.

The speaker-focused approach to campaign finance offers an array of conclusions: spending limits might be completely impermissible; courts might determine for themselves whether the legislature has set limits that allow 'enough' spending; or courts might defer to legislative judgments about possibilities and risks and apply a standard of reasonableness to the legislated limits. A listener-focused approach probably eliminates the first of those conclusions, which might count in favor of taking such an approach, while preserving the second and third. The reason is that a listener-focused approach directs attention immediately to the question of how much spending is enough to ensure that all that is worth saying is said.

Regulation of campaign financing raises a host of additional issues. Some will come up again, such as how to assess such regulation as a form of content-neutral regulation and how to deal with public financing of campaigns. The discussion here has the limited but important aim of comparing speaker- and listener-focused approaches, and ends with the limited but important conclusion that a listener-focused approach has some advantages over a speaker-focused one.

3.5 Conclusion

Those who advocate proportionality as an alternative to more categorical approaches sometimes contend that the distinction between coverage and protection does not arise within proportionality. As suggested in this chapter, that might not be so. And, thinking about the distinction exposes important questions about the structure of free expression law.

4 Rights versus rights/rights versus interests

4.1 Introduction

The treatment of hate speech in the United States differs dramatically from its treatment elsewhere. To overstate only slightly: In the United States regulation of hate speech is constitutionally prohibited, whereas elsewhere its regulation is constitutionally required. Most often scholars attribute the difference to the use of proportionality approaches to free expression law outside the United States and to the use of categorical approaches within the United States. There is, though, another difference in the doctrinal architecture: In the United States the regulation of hate speech poses a conflict between a right (of free expression) and a 'mere' interest (in social equality), whereas elsewhere it poses a conflict between two rights. Doctrinally, when rights confront rights, some sort of balancing or proportionality analysis is required even in the United States, and when rights confront mere interests, the rights prevail categorically (or almost so) even in systems committed to proportionality. We first examine a rights-versus-rights conflict in US law – the so-called 'free press/fair trial' problem, to show how balancing or proportionality ideas operate in such conflicts. The chapter then turns to problems of hate speech, libel, and privacy in US constitutional law and elsewhere (primarily in Europe), to bring out the difference between rights-versus-rights problems and rights-versus-interests ones. It concludes with a brief discussion of the way in which issues of state action or horizontal effect might affect the treatment of rights-versus-interests problems.[1]

---

1 The analysis in this chapter applies as well to the regulation of sexually explicit speech that falls outside the narrow category of obscenity (conventionally, 'pornography'). For a relevant discussion, see Chapter 3.

4.2   Rights versus rights: the free press/fair trial problem

Publishing information about a sensational criminal case can make it more difficult for the defendant to obtain a fair trial: Jurors or other participants in the trial might receive information that they should not; public sentiment can be enflamed in ways that affect prosecutors' decisions.[2] Law-makers, both legislators and judges, have responded by imposing restrictions on what can be published. Outside the setting of criminal trials, though, those restrictions would rather clearly violate freedom of expression. Consider information about a defendant's prior criminal record. In the United States, that information is frequently withheld from the jury, on the theory that knowing it might lead jurors to decide to punish the defendant for his prior misbehavior rather than for the crime at hand. A judge might order newspapers to refrain from publishing that information while the trial is going on, to ensure that jurors will not learn it either inside or outside the courtroom. It would clearly be impermissible to prohibit the media from *ever* publishing that information, for example, in historical accounts of the crime.

The reason that the ban might be permissible while the trial is pending is that its publication then might adversely affect the defendant's ability to obtain a fair trial, which is itself a constitutional right. The problem is one in which one right – the defendant's right to a fair trial – conflicts with another right, the media's right to publish true information. When such problems arise, the solution is straight-forward. In the United States, the formulation is that the rights have to be balanced against each other; where the language of proportionality is used, the formulation, drawn from Robert Alexy, is that the rights have to be (jointly) optimized: We want to get as much of one as we can without having too large an adverse effect upon the other.[3]

Those formulations are not completely adequate, though, because the result of the balancing or optimization will depend on which right one starts with. It is one thing to say that we should have as much

---

2 For ease of exposition the discussion refers to 'jurors' and the like, taking US criminal trials as the core image. The problems affect other forms in which criminal trials occur, though sometimes to different degrees.

3 We might see the problem slightly differently: If the press publishes material that prejudices the defendant's constitutional right to a fair trial, the (only) constitutionally permissible remedy is dismissing the prosecution. That does preserve both rights, but at a potentially high cost to public safety.

information published as is possible without adversely affecting the trial's fairness, another to say that we should have as fair a trial as is possible without limiting too much the media's ability to publish information. US law privileges the media, by requiring judges to exhaust other ways of ensuring fairness before imposing publication bans.[4] Other systems might privilege the defendant, by giving judges broad powers to limit publication of information about the case. In a Canadian case involving murder, rape, and torture, the judge issued a broad injunction against publishing information about the crimes. (The injunction was ineffective because the same information was available within Canada from broadcasts by US television stations.)

One basis for choice between these approaches might be that the adverse effect of publication is focused on one specific individual, the defendant, who might suffer a quite substantial loss when denied a fair trial, whereas the adverse effect of a publication ban is distributed across the public generally, depriving it of one or a few specific items of information that might have some bearing on its understanding of the problem of criminal and criminal justice – a loss that might be thought less substantial than that suffered by the criminal defendant.

So far we have considered case-specific conflicts between freedom of expression and the right to a fair trial. The decision-maker in case-specific conflicts is the individual judge, who has available to her a great deal of information about the specific facts of the case and of the likely forms of publication and distribution of information. In the first instance, case-specific balancing or joint optimization is conceptually relatively easy in such settings. Yet, the judge presiding over the criminal trial might not perform the balancing well enough: She might be invested in doing her best to ensure that any conviction obtained will hold up on appeal against challenges based upon unfair publicity, and so might 'over-protect' the defendant's rights and 'under-protect' the press's. Perhaps, then, higher courts should police this risk not simply by reviewing the balancing on a case-by-case basis, but by developing guidelines and presumptions that trial judges should follow. For example, one guideline might be that the judge must explicitly find that no measures other than the ones she chooses would adequately protect the defendant's interests. Once again, the analysis is second-order in form, concerned about potential errors in making the first-level decision (here, balancing one right against another).

---

4 Richmond Newspapers v. Virginia, 448 U.S. 555 (1980).

General rules to deal with rights conflicts in advance present a different problem. Such rules are rare in the present context, but one can imagine that a legislature, seeking to ensure the fairness of trials for terrorism, might prohibit publication of any information not introduced at a criminal trial. Here the decision-maker is the legislature, which has information about terrorism prosecutions in the aggregate. The analysis of such statutes tracks that laid out in Chapter 1.4: The legislature is assessing risks rather than immediately impending harms, and we should ask whether the assessment is reasonable, taking into account the aggregate effect of the publication ban.

4.3   Rights versus interests: an introduction

Suppose a legislature prohibits the publication of the names of undercover police agents or spies. It might do so because it believes that publishing the names might make it more difficult to conduct undercover operations.[5] For present purposes we can assume that the effective conduct of undercover operations is an important social interest but does not directly implicate anyone's constitutional rights in the way that adverse effects on criminal trials implicate a defendant's constitutional rights. (The word 'directly' matters because crime does adversely affect interests in life and property, although the threats to those interests come from criminals, not the government – and that, as we will see, makes a difference for constitutional analysis.)

The right of free expression of course comes into play if the legislature bans publishing spies' names. Here there is a conflict between a right – of free expression – and a 'mere' interest, in investigating and suppressing crime. Much legislation is justified by mere interests, in the sense that the legislation's goal is to advance the public good generally. Another way of putting the point, which has slightly different implications, is that mere interests are goals governments may pursue but are not constitutionally obligated to pursue.

The word 'mere' does not mean that the interests are unimportant, but only that they are not directly bound up with constitutional rights or duties. Indeed, one might distinguish between statutes that

---

5   A ban justified on the ground that publication would endanger the agents' lives poses a slightly different question, better analyzed with the tools developed in succeeding sections of this chapter. And, of course, the defendant might have a fair-trial right to information about the agents.

pursue constitutionally inflected interests and other statutes. The idea that there might be constitutionally inflected statutes is tied closely to the proposition that constitutional rights are protected only against interference *by the government* – the 'state action' requirement in US law or the similar proposition that constitutional provisions do not have direct horizontal effect. A statute prohibiting race or gender discrimination in employment does not protect constitutional rights, because, as private actors, employers who discriminate cannot violate the constitution. Such a statute could be called constitutionally inflected, though, because it seeks to advance the same value – equality – that the constitutional prohibition on government action denying equality does. Scholars in the United States have discussed how identifying a category of constitutionally inflected statutes might affect constitutional doctrine, but US courts have not yet followed their advice.[6] Were such a category to be recognized, its doctrinal effect in the current context is reasonably clear: Rights-versus-constitutionally-inflected-interests conflicts would be treated as rights-versus-rights conflicts, with a balancing or proportionality test applied.

When the pursuit of an interest impairs a constitutional right – that is, in rights-versus-interests conflicts – there is a strong presumption that the right should prevail. Some of Alexy's formulations can be read to assert that joint optimization is appropriate when rights-versus-interests conflicts arise, but those formulations have been subjected to well-founded criticisms. Joint optimization in rights-versus-interest settings treats constitutional rights as nothing more than really important interests, and that does not give them their due.

The presumption that rights prevail over interests can be overcome. Here a blend of language drawn from US categorical analysis and proportionality analysis is helpful. The presumption in favor of rights in rights-versus-interests conflicts can be overcome if the interest is an extremely important ('compelling') one and the restriction imposed on free expression is not greater than necessary to protect that interest ('narrowly tailored' or 'minimally impairing'). This doctrinal structure does not dictate results: The presumption in favor of free expression might (or might not) be overcome in the case of the 'no publication of spies' names' statute. But, as we will see next, the doctrinal structure

---

6 For an introduction, see John A. Ferejohn and William Eskridge, A Republic of Statutes: The New American Constitution (New Haven: Yale University Press, 2010).

helps us understand some differences between the US and other analyses of several important problems.

4.4   Rights versus interests in the United States and elsewhere: hate speech and libel law

Hate speech undermines the civic equality of its targets; libel impairs the reputation of *its* targets. Prohibiting hate speech enhances civic equality; imposing liability for libelous statements protects reputation and privacy. These are worthy goals. But, in the United States they are mere interests. Although there is a (badly described) right of privacy in the United States, that right deals with decisional autonomy, not control over personal information. Nor is there a free-standing right to civic equality in the United States, but only a requirement that governments take no action to impair civic equality with respect to specific groups.[7] Governments in the United States have no duty to protect personal privacy understood as informational privacy, nor to guard civic equality from threats emanating from private actors. In the central cases the impairments of civic equality and reputation do not arise, in the first instance (an important qualification, as we will see below), from the government itself. Of course governments often choose to protect or promote those interests, and often do so in settings where no questions about free expression could be raised. Because regulations of hate speech and libelous statements impair free expression, we have – again, in the United States – a rights-versus-interests conflict. That regulation requires strong justification.

Few dispute that advancing civic equality is a strong ('compelling', again) public interest. Broad laws against hate speech and restricting libel typically founder, though, on the requirement that they be narrowly tailored. With respect to regulation of hate speech, the most common difficulty is that hate speech is defined both broadly and vaguely, which leaves substantial discretion to those invoking the regulations. And, as we have seen already with respect to libel law, discretion in decision-makers can cause chilling effects substantial enough to worry about. An institutional feature of US law enforcement matters as well: Criminal law enforcement in the United States (as well as private enforcement of libel law) is widely dispersed. Were hate speech laws

---

7   Put another way, in the United States the Constitution guarantees formal equality, not substantive equality. See Chapter 4.5.

to be widely adopted, hundreds if not thousands of prosecutors would have discretion over instituting charges, making selective and discriminatory enforcement a real possibility. Again, the chilling effects could be substantial.

The picture outside the United States is different. Sometimes law enforcement is more concentrated, either generally or with respect to hate speech specifically. Hate speech prosecutions might require approval by a single central authority, as in the United Kingdom, or by a handful of high officials, as in Canada. More importantly, though, outside the United States hate speech and libel law present rights-versus-rights conflicts. Sometimes the right to civic equality is guaranteed in terms, sometimes it is guaranteed indirectly by defining civic equality in outcome-based or substantive terms. Libel law and other forms of protecting a right to privacy understood as control over personal information are even clearer illustrations, because the privacy rights are typically guaranteed in terms in applicable constitutional documents. The end-point, whether reached through explicit texts or constitutional interpretation, is that regulation of hate speech and libel is subject to a balancing or proportionality test rather than a requirement of strong justification.[8]

Another consideration arises when hate speech is banned because its very utterance inflicts harm on civic equality. On this account hate speech is harmful not because it causes any observable action in the world, but because it affects the way its targets are viewed in the community. But, without careful limitation, arguments that allow regulation without a showing of any harm – that allow regulation merely upon utterance – could range quite broadly. For example, one could recast classical sedition law as imposing liability for statements that by their very utterance undermine national unity. And, one might wonder why civic equality among all citizens should be regarded as more important than national unity, such that regulation of hate speech is constitutionally permissible but not regulation of seditious speech. (Indeed, one might wonder whether 'national unity' is even different from 'civic equality among all citizens'.) If there is an answer, it might be that national unity, even understood as implicating civic equality, cannot be fairly described as a right located in any individual. Another

---

8 In explaining the different treatment of hate speech in the United States and elsewhere the structure of legal doctrine is relevant but probably much less significant than cultural and political differences.

possibility, which again might merely be a restatement of the preceding point, is that the harm of hate speech is concentrated on its targets while the harm of seditious speech is distributed across the nation as a whole. Whether that distinction is strong enough to support a rule allowing hate speech regulation but not seditious speech is unclear.

When conflicts between free expression and personal privacy or civic equality are rights-versus-rights conflicts, national law can give free expression *too much* protection. The European Court of Human Rights held, for example, that the German Constitutional Court violated Princess Caroline von Hannover's right to privacy when it denied her claim against press outlets that published pictures of her and her family on vacation.[9] That result is impossible under US law.

4.5   Additional considerations

One might think constitutions with a general right to liberty or a right to the development of the personality or some other right that extends across an extensive range of human activity could dispense with the distinction between rights-versus-rights and rights-versus-interests conflicts. In such constitutional systems, nearly every conflict will be a rights-versus-rights one, with specific rights – in our context, the right of free expression – conflicting with the general right to liberty or the right to development of the personality. Nearly every case would then call for balancing or proportionality analysis.

This is true in some sense, but the rights-versus-interests problem will arise in a different guise. Many conflicts will pit freedom of expression against what some analysts call peripheral aspects of the general right to liberty or the right to development of the personality. For the German Constitutional Court, actually making works of art is at the core of the right of artistic expression, while the right to exhibit it as the artist chooses is not.[10] The right to development of the personality includes the right to pursue one's chosen hobbies, for example, but that right is usually treated as a peripheral example of the core right to development of the personality. Consider then a regulation that

---

9 Von Hannover v. Germany, [2004] ECtHR 294.

10 The case is described in Richard Stacey, 'The Magnetism of Moral Reasoning and the Principle of Proportionality in Comparative Constitutional Adjudication', American Journal of Comparative Law (forthcoming 2018).

requires newspapers to make advertising space available at no cost to associations of stamp collectors (or to associations of people who collect butterflies and all other hobbyists' associations). The regulation impairs the newspapers' free expression right. One could work through the proportionality analysis, but most who do so would conclude, without much difficulty, that the impairment of the free expression right is disproportionate to the incremental advantage given the peripheral aspect of the right to development of the personality. The result is that conflicts between free expression rights and peripheral aspects of general rights look a great deal like rights-versus-interests conflicts, with the modest but perhaps important reservation that sometimes a substantial advantage given to the peripheral right could be proportionate to a relatively small impairment of free expression. Yet, we should recall that that reservation does not operate as an always desirable escape valve, allowing the invalidation of laws that impair free expression only slightly while advancing some peripheral right to a significant degree. The reason, as discussed earlier, is that courts invoking the doctrine in such cases may mistakenly conclude that a serious impairment of free expression is only a minor one, or that a minor benefit to the peripheral right is a substantial one.

4.6   Private versus public impairments of interests

The difference between US law and the law elsewhere, as we have seen, results in part from the fact that under US law hate speech and libelous statements implicate mere interests – in equality and private life – whereas elsewhere such statements implicate competing rights in equality, privacy, and the right to free development of the personality.

Some supporters of hate speech laws describe them in rights-versus-rights terms. Hate speech, they argue, has the effect of 'silencing' its targets, sometimes by deterring targets from participating in public life, sometimes by creating a culture in which the views expressed by targets are given less weight than they would otherwise have. Characterized in this way, hate speech laws might be seen as a method to maximize speech: The reduction in speech by users of hate speech is more than offset by the increase of speech by their targets. Chapter 5 discusses how free expression law deals with legislation aimed at maximizing speech. Its conclusion is that such legislation is ordinarily reviewed generously, through a test of reasonableness. So, one might think, hate speech laws understood as speech-maximizing efforts would be permissible if reasonable.

Yet, recasting hate speech as a problem of speech-maximizing runs up against the difficulty that one source of speech restriction is the government (through hate speech regulation) while the other sources are private actors (those engaging in hate speech). Many constitutional systems deny that constitutional provisions apply to private actors. This is the 'state action' rule in the United States: Constitutional provisions apply only when the government is acting. It is the denial of horizontal effect to constitutional provisions elsewhere. Those engaging in hate speech do not violate the free expression rights of their targets, when those rights are understood in state action terms as immunities from government regulation.

The same can be said of equality as impaired by hate speech and security of private life as impaired by libelous statements. Hate speech might impair the targets' equal standing in the community, but the impairment results from actions by private actors, not the government. Similarly with the intrusion on privacy and personality caused by libelous statements. They too emanate from private actors. Another way of putting the same point is that under US law governments have no constitutional duty to promote equality or personal privacy, although they frequently choose to do so.

These points immediately suggest an important legal and rhetorical strategy. The analytic framework changes dramatically if we shift from a rights-versus-interests conflict to a rights-versus-rights one. The strong presumption in favor of free expression is replaced by a balancing test under which regulation is more easily justified. The strategy then is to transform a mere interest into a right. That is the intuition underlying the 'silencing' argument, but that argument fails because of the state action/no horizontal effect rule. Rather, we must devise some way of transforming what private actors say, their hate speech or libelous statements, into governmental action.

Though cast in somewhat different terms, Jeremy Waldron's recent analysis of hate speech regulation points in this direction.[11] Waldron argues that hate speech regulation is permissible as a means for promoting civic equality when the general social environment is per-

---

11 Jeremy Waldron, The Harm in Hate Speech (Cambridge, MA: Harvard University Press, 2012).

vaded by images and messages denying that hate speech's targets are full citizens and participants in civic life. That environment results from actions by private actors employing the resources they have as they choose. But, the argument would go, they have those resources because of legal entitlements – because of state action. Were those entitlements to be different, some purveyors of hate speech would find doing so much more difficult. So, by adjusting entitlements the government can affect the overall social environment. Where equality provisions have direct or indirect horizontal effect, for example, employers cannot refuse to hire someone because of her gender, whether because they are directly bound by the constitution or because the constitution affects the interpretation of their 'ordinary' right to select employees according to their own criteria.

Importantly, the adjustment cannot take the form of denying a right to use one's property to disseminate hate speech; that would be a regulation of speech and therefore subject to ordinary constitutional analysis. Rather, the adjustment must be in the law of contract and property itself. One creative (and implausible, in the real world) possibility would be to give members of classes typically the target of hate speech a general right to veto exercises of property and contract rights by nonmembers of those classes. This would be a regulation of property and contract in the service of equality, not a regulation of speech.

Constitutional systems have the resources to get around the state action/no horizontal effect doctrine. Were those resources to be used, they could transform rights-versus-interests conflicts into rights-versus-rights ones. The analytic moves are quite subtle, though, and few scholars – and even fewer legislators – appear willing to use the resources as they would have to be used.

These analytic moves are unnecessary where governments already have a constitutional duty to advance equality. Such a duty flows from a constitutional commitment to equality understood substantively rather than procedurally. Substantive equality focuses on outcomes or distributions. Outcomes and distributions can result in part from choices by private actors. To the extent that they do, a government required to ensure substantive equality must do something to adjust the outcomes. That is precisely what happens when hate speech confronts substantive equality: A rights-versus-rights conflict arises, and a balance must be struck.

4.7   The special problem of copyright

Copyright law is – in theory – designed to encourage people to produce expression: Without the economic incentive provided by copyright protection, some people would find it more valuable to spend their time doing something else than writing books or publishing pamphlets. Yet, copyright law is enforced by *suppressing* expression – prohibiting people who copy material from distributing it. What is copyright's place within the general structure of free expression law?

One unpromising approach is to treat copyright as a categorical exception to free expression law. In the United States this sometimes takes the form of asserting that copyright law cannot violate the First Amendment because it is a form of property expressly authorized by the Constitution, which gives Congress the power 'to promote the Progress of Science and useful Arts, by securing for limited Times to Authors . . . the exclusive Right to their . . . Writings . . .'. Citing the Copyright Clause cannot advance the argument, though. Exercises of every other congressional power are constrained by the First Amendment: Congress could not exercise its power to regulate interstate commerce by banning the distribution of books attacking Republicans (or Democrats) across state lines. The same is true of the Copyright Clause: Congress cannot exercise its power to 'secure rights in writings' in a way that violates the First Amendment.

A variant of this argument, relevant to copyright law not only in the United States, is that copyright is a property right. Enforcing it by suppressing expression, it might be thought, creates a rights-versus-rights conflict, with the right to property conflicting with the right to free expression. Describing the problem in this way is a mistake, because the constitutional right to property is a quite limited one: It is a right to compensation when property is 'taken', in the US formulation (the constitutional right to property in other constitutional systems is typically even more limited). The US Supreme Court has defined 'taking' as depriving the property owner of all economic value in the property. Consider now some copyright infringement that does deprive the author of all economic value – a complete reprinting of the work on cheaper paper, for example. A government decision that such an appropriation was lawful probably should be understood as a *government* taking of the property – the exercise by the infringer of a power it has under law to take the work away from the author.

Harper & Row v. Nation provides a helpful illustration.[12] Harper & Row, a publisher, had a contract to publish Gerald Ford's memoirs. *Time* magazine agreed to pay the publisher for an exclusive right to publish excerpts from the memoir, which, the magazine assumed, would include Ford's account of his controversial decision to pardon Richard Nixon. *The Nation*, another magazine, got hold of an advance copy of the memoir and published excerpts, including the treatment of the pardon. As a result, *Time* canceled its contract with the publisher, depriving the publisher of $12,500 due on the contract. Harper & Row sued *The Nation* for that amount. *The Nation* asserted that the First Amendment required that what it had done be treated as 'fair use' protected by the Copyright Act. The Supreme Court disagreed. Among the reasons the Court gave for not treating the use as 'fair' was that *The Nation*'s publication effectively destroyed the economic value associated with what it called 'first serialization rights'.

We might use a metaphor from property law here. *The Nation*'s action completely destroyed one of the important 'sticks' in the bundle of sticks that together make up copyright seen as a property right. And, as we will see in Chapter 6.4, we might treat a statute that protected what *The Nation* did as fair use might be treated as a taking of that stick from the bundle. Many copyright infringements do not come close to this sort of complete appropriation of an economically significant component of the work's value; they are at most the equivalent of a modest regulatory taking for which compensation would not generally be owed. In these settings, then, copyright is an interest (copyright as regulable property)-versus-rights (free expression) conflict.

Seen in that way, we would have to ask how strong was the government interest in promoting knowledge by giving authors the economic incentives copyright provides. That copyright does give some authors some incentives is of course true, Still, observing how much material is produced by people who simply want to get their ideas out to the public, and who do not need an economic incentive to do so, we might wonder whether the government interest is strong enough to satisfy a requirement that the interest be strong (or 'compelling' and the like).

In a rights-versus-interests conflict, rules that protect the interests have to be carefully drawn or 'narrowly tailored'. In upholding an extension of copyright protection, the US Supreme Court described several features

---

12 471 U.S. 539 (1985).

of copyright law as 'First Amendment safeguards': the distinction between unprotectable ideas and protected expression, and the ability of others to make 'fair use' of copyrighted materials, including the right to parody the original material. The implication is that, at the very least, it is possible to create copyright as a 'mere' property interest in ways that allow some copyright protection without violating free expression law.

Another approach might be more promising. We might see the problem as a rights-versus-rights problem, with the author's free expression right conflicting with the infringer's free expression right. Put another way, we might see copyright as a problem *within* free expression, not between free expression and something else. Copyright law encourages but also suppresses expression. Economists might say that we have a problem of 'joint optimization': We want to get as much expression as possible with as little suppression as possible. Suppress too little speech – allow too many limitations on copyright – and we will not get as much speech as we would get if we suppressed more speech: The increase in speech through strong copyright protection exceeds the decrease in speech suppressed by such protection. The obverse problem is obvious: We might suppress too much speech without getting an offsetting increase in speech produced because of copyright's incentives.

Easy enough to state in principle; however, the 'joint optimization' idea is difficult to pin down in particulars. In this it resembles other speech-versus-speech problems such as the true heckler's veto one (Section 5.4). Here as there, the answer might be that law-makers should have a fairly wide range of discretionary choice.

4.8 Conclusion

Some observations about history and culture seem appropriate in conclusion. The US Constitution is a document framed in the eighteenth and mid-nineteenth centuries, and reflects ideas about the proper scope of government that prevailed then. European and other constitutions were framed in the twentieth and twenty-first centuries, and reflect the rather different ideas about the proper scope of government then prevailing. In a phrase, the US Constitution is a liberal document; European constitutions are social democratic documents. The doctrinal differences examined in this chapter are expressions of that difference.

5 Subsidies and content-neutral regulations

5.1 Introduction

The discussion to this point has dealt almost entirely with regulations of speech based on its content. The reason is that judicial and scholarly consideration of content-based regulation began early and has been sustained at a sophisticated level for decades if not centuries. For just as long, though, there have been other forms of political protest – demonstrations and riots in the streets. Until the twentieth century free expression law said nothing about that form of expression – or, more accurately, regarded regulation of street demonstrations as entirely discretionary. Governments could allow demonstrations, regulate them however they chose, or ban them entirely. In one formulation, the government owned the streets and like any property owner had the power to do whatever it wanted with them.

The twentieth century saw the development of a law of free expression dealing with public demonstrations. The reasons are not entirely clear. One may have been a growing understanding on the part of governments that demonstrations were inevitable and that regulating them was more likely to promote social stability than banning them. Another may have been concern that demonstrations were one of the few modes of expression that people without many resources could easily use. These reasons, though, would support policy choices to regulate demonstrations, but they do not obviously support constitutional limits on such regulation.

Initially scholars and then courts concluded that free expression law required that such demonstrations be allowed but that reasonable 'time, place, and manner' regulations of demonstrations were consistent with free expression. Further consideration led to the conclusion, now widely accepted, that time, place, and manner regulations were a subset of a larger category of 'content-neutral' regulations, that is, of regulations imposed across the board to all instances of expression no matter what the speaker said.

The structure of doctrine dealing with content-neutral regulations brings out the fact that free expression law involves a range of subsidies for expression. Sometimes the subsidies flow from the general public to the speaker and can be understood as something like a tax required by the constitutional protection given free expression. More problematically, sometimes the subsidies flow to the speaker from a single individual or from a small class. The law dealing with content-based regulations brings to the surface contrasts between categorical and proportionality approaches to constitutional analysis; the law dealing with content-neutral regulations brings to the surface contrasts between constitutions understood as limitations on government powers – negative constitutions – and constitutions as vehicles for requiring the enhancement of individual liberty – positive constitutions.

5.2   Basic rules about regulating demonstrations

As noted, one important reason for allowing but regulating street demonstrations is that doing so might be in the government's interest. Sometimes free expression law is explained with reference to the fact that allowing speech (subject to regulation) is a 'safety valve' against more violent forms of opposition to the government. Speech subject to regulation allows dissidents to let off steam that might otherwise build up to an explosion. The 'safety valve' account is puzzling in two dimensions. From the dissidents' point of view, it seems condescending: The government is saying that it will permit the speech precisely because it does not pose a serious threat (and suggests that speech will be permitted up to the point where it does pose such a threat). And, from the government's point of view, the 'safety valve' account invokes an interest the government itself has, which makes it somewhat puzzling to subject the government's choices to constitutional scrutiny: If the government wants a safety valve, it is free to allow speech at its discretion, and if it chooses not to allow the speech, that choice could be taken as evidence that the government believes that no safety valve is needed (for example, because even if suppressed the speech would not lead to a dangerous build-up of pressure).

Perhaps, though, governments are prone to mistakes about when a safety valve is needed. They may misestimate their own interests because, perhaps, they overestimate their ability to control explosive outbursts. They might erroneously believe that they have the resources – police forces, primarily – to control those outbursts if they occur, or at least might underestimate the social costs of using force. Or, they might refuse to allow demonstrations selectively: Government supporters can hold marches but not government opponents. In a reasonably democratic society that selectivity is troubling because it may make it easier for the government to hold on to power. Doctrinally, this concern is captured by the idea that discretionary power can be exercised in a way that discriminates among viewpoints (here, pro- and anti-government views).

If the government must allow demonstrations in the streets but can regulate them, what form can the regulation take? There are many possibilities, and here we focus on a rather simple set of regulations to bring out the deeper points about how free expression law operates as a subsidy. Consider a medium-sized city with a central business district downtown, one large park near downtown, and several other parks scattered around the city. A group interested in getting its message across through a peaceful march or demonstration decides that the most effective ones would be a march through downtown at rush hour, and a demonstration at the main city park on a weekend afternoon. City officials make a reasonable judgment that those activities would be extremely disruptive: The march would interfere with the flow of traffic at a crucial time of day, and the demonstration would make it more difficult for families to use the park for their customary recreational weekend activities. Rather than deny the group the opportunity to march and demonstrate, though, the officials offer several alternatives: The group can march downtown in the afternoon but must complete the march before rush hour begins, or they can have a march several blocks away during rush hour; it can use the main city park for its demonstration on a weekday, or it can use one of the city's other parks for a weekend demonstration.

Free expression law almost everywhere would allow the officials to regulate the march and demonstration in these ways. That is so, importantly, even though the alternatives they make available to the group are less effective in getting the group's message across (that is, even though the group is correct in thinking that their message would have its largest audience at the times and places it proposes). The reason for allowing these regulations is three-fold: the justifications for the regulations have nothing to do with the content of the proposed march and demonstration; the regulations provide the group with adequate though not perfect alternatives; and the regulations are reasonable. Note that the doctrinal test incorporates deference to reasonable judgments by political officials and thus responds directly to the central idea introduced in Chapter 1.

We can contrast these regulations with unreasonable ones (for example, a strict and low limit on the number of marchers) and with ones that do not offer adequate alternatives (for example, allowing the demonstration only late at night). The idea of content-neutrality is what traditional formulations sought to capture in the phrase 'time, place, and manner', but it is content-neutrality that matters.

The reasons for upholding regulations of marches and demonstrations conceal a number of difficulties.

(a)   Symbolically important spaces

Suppose a group proposes to hold a demonstration in a symbolically important space. These might include a square in front of the nation's parliament building, a square closely associated with national independence, an open space near a jail where a prominent dissenter is being held, or the publicly owned parking lot surrounding a public arena where a political convention is being held. Demonstrations in these venues might raise distinct concerns about security, going beyond the general concern that demonstrations disrupt the ordinary flow of things through the public spaces. Evaluating the security claim may be difficult because, on the one hand, the security threat may indeed be more substantial than elsewhere, but on the other, officials have an incentive both to overestimate the security threat and to control information bearing on that threat: They might overestimate the risk that a demonstration will turn violent and threaten the parliament building itself, or the candidates accepting a nomination, or the physical integrity of the jail. Proportionality analysis seems well-suited to deal with this problem.

As is typical, the US law of free expression is more categorical about the spaces that must be made available. It distinguishes among traditional public spaces ('public forums', in doctrinal terms), such as streets and parks, dedicated public forums such as publicly owned arenas and theaters, and non-public forums, whose primary use has almost nothing to do with communications, such as a jailhouse. Public forums can be allocated according to the general rule about reasonably available alternatives, as must – in general – dedicated public forums. Non-public forums need not be made available at all, but if they are, access to them must be provided without regard to the viewpoints of those seeking access.

That the distinction between categorical and proportionality approaches is less sharp than one might think can be brought out by considering a dedicated public forum – a public theater used for performances of plays and music. Is the theater *dedicated* to plays, so that the government can refuse to allow a political group to rent it when no performance is scheduled to occur? Can the government dedicate the theater to 'family friendly' plays, so that it can refuse to allow a politically charged or sexually explicitly play to be performed there? What if the jailhouse is not a free-standing structure, but merely a part of a larger municipal building? The gap between a categorical approach and proportionality analysis can be narrowed by increasingly refined characterizations of the venues involved.

(b)   Reasonable alternatives and disparate impact

As presented, the domain of reasonable alternatives is public space – one street or park rather than another. An emerging issue is whether the domain should expand to include social media. Could a government deny access to *any* public space at all, or to some specific space without offering an alternative, on the ground that the group seeking to use the space has a reasonable alternative in social media? Professor Cass Sunstein once suggested that access to public spaces makes the group's message available to unexpected passers-by whereas on social media people encounter only (or mostly) those with whom they already agree. This is an empirical claim on both sides (how many unexpected encounters are there in connection with both the social media and marches and demonstrations?), which deserves investigation.

The development of social media as a means of communication might affect the law of marches and demonstrations on a deeper level. Denying access to public spaces for such activities relegates groups to the private sector when they want to organize and communicate. They would have to rent a meeting hall, for example, or pay radio and television stations to spread their messages. Yet, obviously, some groups – call them the relatively well-to-do – have more resources to spend in these private markets than poorer people. One rationale for constitutionally guaranteed access to streets and parks for expressive activity is that such access is the poor person's method of communicating a message and organizing supporters. Assuming as most scholars do that poor people have different views from richer ones on many policy issues, constitutionally guaranteed access responds to the disparate impact of relying entirely on markets to allocate opportunities to communicate.

Access to social media is cheap enough that their availability might offset the disparate impact of private markets to a substantial extent. In a phrase, it might well be easier to organize a 'flash mob' via social media than a traditional street march or demonstration. Of course flash mobs themselves use public spaces, so the phrase is not entirely accurate. The underlying point, though, is that communicating views through the social media, to those who already support those views and perhaps to those who do not (yet), may now be a reasonably effective alternative to using streets and parks for those purposes. No court appears yet to have adopted this view, though.

(c)   Content-neutrality and disparate impact

That a march will disrupt traffic is a content-neutral reason for regulating it. What if the amount of disruption is correlated, as it almost always will be, with the content of the marcher's message? In some places a march supporting vegetarianism will attract only a handful of marchers and observers; the traffic disruption will be small; and it might be unreasonable to deny the marchers access to a main thoroughfare for several hours. Elsewhere the same march would attract an extremely large group of supporters (and opponents), and the traffic disruption would be large. The question then is whether invoking traffic disruption as a justification for denying the group access to the main street should be treated as content-neutral. Put another way, some regulations that are content-neutral on their face – justifying regulations with reference to traffic disruption, in the example – have a disparate impact depending upon the content of the speech at issue.

This difficulty may be exacerbated when one suspects, again as may often be the case, that officials implicitly or unconsciously take content into account in applying facially neutral justifications. The solution, if there is one, is to require (1) that the justifications be developed in advance of any specific march or demonstration, which might be captured in a requirement that the regulations occur 'by law' rather than ad hoc, and (2) that the justifications take as objective a form as possible, for example, by measuring potential traffic disruption with reference solely to the number of marchers expected (and perhaps even by giving the march organizers input on the question of how many people they expect to show up).

Free expression law in the United States has circled around this solution. The solution has a categorical flavor, particularly in its disregard of seemingly relevant facts, such as that some messages will elicit opposition, and that the number of opponents may not be as easy to estimate as the number of marchers. Proportionality analysis applied after the events would take the actual facts into account, and applied before it would require an assessment of officials' estimates about a wide range of facts. A categorical approach almost certainly restricts regulators' discretion more than a proportionality approach would, and in the present context that might well be desirable. Note, once again, that the defense of the categorical approach is institutional: It asks not what the best or most reasonable regulations of the march are (or were), but what is the best way to limit discretionary decisions that, we might worry, would be based implicitly or unconsciously on the basis of content or might have a disparate and anticipated disparate content-based effect.

(d)   Subsidies

Even reasonable regulations of marches and demonstrations impose some costs. Businesses along the parade route may attract fewer customers than they ordinarily would at the same hours; commuters attempting to cross the line of march will be delayed; families seeking to relax in their preferred park will have to find something else to do or some other park to go to. Seeing these costs from the other side brings out the fact that free expression law here is not merely a ban on government actions that restrict speech opportunities, but constitutes a subsidy to expression.

One might quarrel with characterizing as a subsidy the costs resulting from constitutionally required government actions such as making streets and parks available for marches and demonstrations. They could be seen instead as the costs of living in a free society. Perhaps so, but seeing them as subsidies provides better leverage in thinking about the size and distribution of those costs.

The costs of making streets and parks available, for example, are distributed broadly among businesses, commuters, and families. Once we see this as a subsidy flowing from those groups to the marchers and demonstrators, we can see subsidies elsewhere. For example, constitutional limitations on recovery through libel law of damages for injury to reputation require specific individuals to subsidize the press in an amount measured by civil damage awards, and constitutional limitations on hate speech require the target groups to subsidize the speakers. Some subsidies might be justified but how the subsidies are extracted might be questioned. The libel subsidy seems questionable because identifiable individuals are forced to subsidize the commercial press because of general benefits to the public; perhaps we should consider the possibility that free expression law should require compensation to injured individuals from general tax funds. The hate speech subsidy might be offset by programs aiding the targeted groups, such as programs of affirmative action or positive discrimination, seen as required by free expression law rather than as options or requirements under equality provisions. Free expression law has nowhere (yet) drawn these conclusions but, again, the perspective offered by the 'subsidy' characterization opens them up for discussion.

That perspective is particularly illuminating in an important area, where marchers and demonstrators confront a hostile audience.

5.3   The problem of the hostile audience

Demonstrations and marches create direct costs to the government, not merely the costs associated with disrupting the spaces' normal uses. Participants may throw away more trash than would otherwise happen, and sanitation workers will have to collect it – perhaps working overtime. Courts and scholars have thought about these excess costs (that is, more than would occur when the spaces were used in their normal ways) primarily in the context of security costs that occur when those who disagree with the demonstrators' views line the streets or surround the park where the demonstration is taking place. The opponents might threaten violence against the demonstrators, and the government has a general duty to protect law-abiding people, including demonstrators, against violence. What does free expression law say about allocating the excess costs associated with marches and demonstrations? We begin with consideration of what government officials can do before a demonstration occurs, then turn to what they must do during the demonstration.

The first step is simple. Officials can require that those planning a demonstration notify them about their proposed time, route, numbers expected to participate, and the like – basic information about how the planners expect or hope the demonstration to unfold. Some systems involve notification followed by interactions between the planners and the government; others involve permit requirements, which, again, are typically developed through interactions and negotiations.

One guideline for these interactions has already been mentioned – a requirement, inevitably loosely enforceable, that the government come up with estimates of the excess costs that are based upon as objective a set of criteria as possible. The reason is that, without such criteria, there is a risk of implicit viewpoint discrimination. Suppose the demonstrators oppose a government policy and their hostile viewers support the policy. One would not be surprised to discover that government officials in charge of estimating excess costs would come up with higher estimates in such a case than in a case where the demonstrators supported government policy. So, for example, the government might have to make good-faith estimates of the overtime it would have to pay sanitation workers to clean up after a demonstration.

Why, though, are we concerned about the accuracy of such estimates? The answer once again lies in concerns about disparate impact. Consider a demonstration against government policies, believed by the demonstrators to be inadequate, addressing human-caused climate change. Suppose as well that the sponsors of the demonstration are relatively well-off. Free expression law as it has developed is not entirely clear about permissible government responses, but there are some suggestions – sensible enough – that the sponsors could be charged a reasonable fee to cover the excess costs of cleaning up after the demonstration. Put another way, the government might have a constitutional duty to subsidize the speech activities of those who cannot afford to get their views across other than through marches and demonstrations, but if a relatively well-to-do group makes a strategic decision to disseminate its views through a demonstration rather than through a radio broadcast, it does not seem unreasonable to ask them to pay the costs associated with that choice, at least to the extent that they can do so. (One might guard against the possibility of biased estimates by allowing the government to require the group to pay only a portion of the good-faith estimated excess costs. This is a second-order rule of a type we have already encountered.)

Excess clean-up costs are one thing. What of excess policing costs? One possibility is that the government must absorb such costs, on the theory mentioned earlier, that one of the government's most essential tasks is protecting law-abiding people against unlawful violence. As stated, that proposition cannot be completely adequate. Consider a demonstration in a small city, with only a small number of police officers, faced with a demonstration that is likely to attract a large number of hostile viewers. Protecting the demonstrators would require the city to deploy all of its police officers to the demonstration – and thereby leave the rest of the city unpatrolled and at risk of criminal activities such as burglary. We might want to say that even this result is the consequence of living in a society with a robust free expression law. Justice Aharon Barak of the Supreme Court of Israel referred to it as 'the natural functions of the police' and 'the price of democracy', tied closely to the constitutional protection given to freedom of expression: 'The duty of the state according to the "positive" aspect of the right of freedom of speech and demonstration means . . . its duty to allow the realization of the right to demonstrate by providing security and maintaining public order during the demonstration.'[1]

Alternatively, we can think of the provision of police services as a subsidy to demonstrators, justified at least in part by concerns about the inability of groups with low resources to get their message across by purchasing advertising. Consider again a group that could afford to rent a private space for its rally and hire private security guards to ensure against violence. As before, it does not seem unreasonable to require the group to pay for the excess police costs (up to the amount it would have paid for private security guards), in light of the group's strategic choice to hold the rally in a public space. Administering a requirement for reimbursement of excess costs of policing (and clean-up) might be difficult, which counsels against rules that demand a great deal either of officials (in determining costs) or demonstrators (in terms of raising money to pay the costs). But, in principle, free expression law should not – and typically does not – require the government (and taxpayers) to absorb all the excess costs associated with demonstrations.

Demonstrations and rallies are fluid events, and often things happen that were not fully anticipated: More marchers show up than had been expected, or, more importantly, more counter-demonstrators show up. The allocation of police resources might have been reasonable before

---

1   Majority Camp v. Israel Police, HCJ 2557/05, 12 Dec. 2006 (Isr.). This opinion and the somewhat less illuminating Forsyth County v. Nationalist Movement, 505 U.S. 123 (1992), are perhaps the best expositions of the problem of the hostile audience.

the event began to unfold, but it might turn out to be inadequate in the circumstances. What does free expression law require or permit when violence breaks out despite the presence of what had been thought beforehand were enough police officers?

The first response must be that the police must do what they can to end the violence by directing their attention to those actually engaging in violence – here, in the first instance, the counter-demonstrators. This flows not merely from the general duty to prevent violence by arresting those who engage in it, but also from the demonstrators' free expression right: If their message is not itself unlawful and if their presence in the space is lawful, free expression requires that the government do what it can to facilitate their communication in the face of violence. If the police are overwhelmed by the counter-demonstrators, they can request that the demonstrators leave and, under extreme circumstances, direct that they do so. Only at the end of this sequence – attempt to protect the speakers, fail to do so, fail to persuade the speakers to leave – may the police arrest the demonstrators. The theory here, perhaps a bit strained but understandable, is that they are not being punished for the speech they made, for their messages, but for disregarding a lawful police demand, where the lawfulness of the demand rests on the violent circumstances.

5.4   The heckler's veto and the role of civil society

The problem of the hostile audience is sometimes misdescribed as involving a 'heckler's veto'. But the heckler's veto is a distinct subcategory of the hostile audience problem. So far we have examined free expression law in connection with violence caused by counter-demonstrators. What, though, if the counter-demonstrators 'merely' heckle the speakers? Heckling can take many forms – occasional outbursts from the audience of 'You lie' through more sustained jeering and booing to the end-point when the speaker is shouted down, in the sense that the speaker cannot get her message across even to those interested in hearing it.

The starting point is that in general those opposing the speaker should be understood as among her audience, lawfully present in the space. Free expression law entitles the speaker to use the public space but does not entitle her to appropriate it for her exclusive use. Nor does the fact that the speaker has a permit or the like give her speech any priority over speech – 'You lie' and jeers – from the audience. They too are exercising their free expression rights.

Few scholars believe that free expression law allows the police to remove someone who interjects at a critical comment, and it is difficult to see what permissible government interest is promoted by allowing them to do so. The same is true of persistent jeering and booing. The speaker is entitled to speak but not entitled to suppress speech by those who disagree, as long as the counter-speakers are lawfully present and not engaged in violence.

Contention arises at the limit case, where the counter-demonstrators effectively shout down the speaker, making it impossible for the speaker to get her message across even to those who are interested in hearing it. Many have a reasonably strong intuition that shouting a speaker down is inconsistent with free expression norms. Whether it is inconsistent with free expression law is less clear. Actual cases in which the government moves against demonstrators who have shouted down a speaker are few. What principle might justify such actions? The best candidate is that the government has some obligation to ensure that speakers who use public spaces are able to communicate their messages with some degree of effectiveness. Yet, there rather clearly is no such obligation in general, and why there should be one in connection with public spaces is unclear.

Perhaps free expression law simply does not address the true heckler's veto: The government may act against counter-demonstrators who shout speakers down, or not, in its discretion. Or, perhaps – contrary to the intuitions just mentioned – free expression law actually protects the heckler's veto, in the sense that the government may not act against counter-demonstrators, who are, after all, exercising their own right of free expression. Or, perhaps, we should think of this as a rights-versus-rights conflict, and resolve it according to some sort of balancing. Balancing typically asks how much resolving the problem in favor of the speaker would enhance the speaker's ability to speak compared to its inhibition of the counter-protestors' ability to speak; and conversely, how much resolving the problem in favor of the counter-demonstrators would enhance their ability to speak compared to its inhibition of the speaker's ability. This might help in some scenarios, as when the speaker is a public official confronted with dissidents (where the balance might favor the counter-speakers), or where the speaker is a quite marginal critic of the government and the audience consists of strong supporters of the government (where the balance might favor the speaker). It is unlikely to be useful when both the speaker and the counter-demonstrators represent minority views. Note as well that in these scenarios the balancing appears to take into account the views expressed, which seems unpromising for institutional reasons of the sort we have recurrently encountered. Some crisp rule, on the order of 'first come, first served' might be better; such a rule would at least authorize and might require the police to remove the counter-demonstrators.

Finally, taking the listener's perspective (Chapter 3.4.2), we might conclude that focusing on the moment of confrontation is a mistake, and that we should ask whether the views expressed during the event are available to listeners in some structured way. Where heckling occurs at one lecture in a series, perhaps we should ask whether the views made available by the series as a whole encompass those to which the heckling is addressed; if they are, an episode of heckling might be overlooked because, in Meiklejohn's terms, all that needs to be said, is said.

As these scenarios indicate, the heckler's veto problem has many variants. What if the speaker is invited by someone who controls access to the space, as in a university? What if the speaker permissibly attempts to control access to the speech? It may be that free expression law is inadequate to deal with all the variants. Rather, we might want to rely on civility norms here. So, for example, in British parliamentary debates speakers are expected to deal with occasional heckling and jeering, but norms of proper conduct inhibit the speaker's opponents from going too far.[2]

We might want to consider the far broader question of the circumstances under which we could use civility norms rather than law to regulate expression. One difficulty with civility norms is that they are likely to inscribe 'political correctness' in a pejorative sense. Norms generally and civility norms specifically tend to be set by the majority and for that reason tend to preserve the status quo. Should those who believe that a government program – the ongoing conduct of a war, for example – is deeply wrong be inhibited by civility norms from expressing their disagreement with the policy in the most forceful

---

2 For an astute analysis, see Jeremy Waldron, 'Heckle: To Disconcert with Questions, Challenges, or Gibes' 2017 Supreme Court Review 1 (2017).

terms? Recall *Cohen v. California*, the 'Fuck the Draft' case. There the Supreme Court rejected the government's assertion that it had the power to regulate the public use of that expletive for the purpose of improving the quality of civic discourse. Civility norms, though, still constrain the word's use. Many newspapers refrain from publishing it because of a civility norm. Yet, when if at all should ordinary citizens be inhibited from using it because of a civility norm? Perhaps the civility norm is something like, 'Don't use the word in public unless it's really important', or, in the heckler's veto setting, 'Don't shout down a speaker unless it's really important'. That *is* something, and indeed it may be enough to vindicate reliance on civility norms rather than law to regulate expression in many contexts.

5.5   Government speech and explicit subsidies

The preceding discussion of speech in public spaces has brought out the way in which free expression law involves implicit subsidies to expression. Sometimes the subsidies are explicit. Governments operate national orchestras and support national art and history museums, for example, and have programs providing funds to artists and writers. They also spend money to disseminate ideas about and defenses of government policy. Many people worry that these programs can turn into normatively troubling government 'propaganda', in which the government uses its enormous tax resources – drawn from the pockets of both supporters and opponents – to entrench highly contested values and, even more, to entrench itself against displacement by opponents. Statutes regulate a great deal of this government 'propaganda' in reasonably well-functioning democracies, largely because it is quite difficult to develop constitutional rules that target only troubling practices without constraining valuable ones.

5.5.1   Government speech

We can array government speech quite crudely along a spectrum ranging from messages supporting widely shared social values, to those supporting more contested ones, to those supporting and encouraging participation in recently enacted (and older) statutes, to those encouraging support for proposed statutes, to those encouraging support for proposals to change the rules of the political game. Examples at each point might be these (drawn mostly from US experience, but with analogies everywhere): 'Racial Harmony Strengthens the Nation', 'Say

No to Drugs', 'Enroll Now in HealthCare', 'Our Education Program Will Enhance Our Economy', 'Amend the Constitution to Prohibit Corporate Spending on Political Campaigns'. As we move along the spectrum people become increasingly uncomfortable about allowing the government to disseminate the messages.

One complexity is that government officials are also politicians, and, as political scientists have long noted, 'new policies make new politics'. That is, a politician proposes some new policy because she believes it will enhance her political position, making it easier for her to gain re-election or for her party to gain seats in the legislature. Even if we regulate *government* speech near the troublesome end of the spectrum we cannot sensibly regulate speech by politicians at the same point: Perhaps the Ministry of Health and its civil service employees can be prohibited from campaigning in favor of a revision in the national health care system, but the Minister of Health cannot. Distinguishing between the Minister's speech in her official capacity and in her political one is quite difficult, and even writing statutes that draw the correct distinctions is difficult (particularly when the Minister's political opponents might make her supposedly illegal actions a political issue). Normative concerns about speech rather far along the spectrum might be addressed directly by politics and norms rather than law. That is, the government's political opponents can make its participation in disseminating what they describe pejoratively as propaganda a political issue, and the fear of political loss may constrain government officials from going 'too far' – as may norms about the use of taxpayers' resources for 'mere' political gain.

Early scholarship on government speech emphasized the possibility that the government might deploy its quite large resources – garnered from taxes imposed on people some of whom disagreed with the government's policies – to 'drown out' competing voices. Today that concern is captured in worries about the government's ability to 'flood' the arena of discussion with so much information as to exhaust citizens' ability to pay attention to the policies at issue. Yet, devising constitutional rules that pin down the idea of 'too much information' is extremely difficult, perhaps impossible. Here too we probably have to rely on organized political opposition within legislatures to place some limits on how much information 'the government' – meaning here the executive branch – can disseminate.[3]

---

3 For additional discussion, see Chapter 6.

Government speech along most of the spectrum is and probably must be at most only loosely regulated by law. Some courts have imposed constitutional limits on government speech at the very end, though, where changes in constitutional rules, particularly those dealing with the political system itself, are at stake. The Irish Supreme Court, for example, held it unconstitutional for the government to spend taxpayer money to support only one side in a referendum campaign to amend the constitution to allow divorce, and the Massachusetts Supreme Court held it unconstitutional for the city of Boston to spend money supporting a referendum to increase taxes on corporations.[4] If these holdings are justified by some basic principle rather than by the specific terms of individual constitutions, it must be that government speech on matters going to the rules of politics itself poses too great a risk of entrenching incumbents against displacement through politics itself.

So far we have considered speech by the government itself – by government ministries and ministers, for example. Governments also hire private actors to disseminate favored views. That practice is problematic when the arrangement is concealed, because those who hear the messages might believe that they are finding out something from private actors and civil society when they are actually hearing what the government wants them to hear. Here too statutes, ordinary politics, and norms must do a great deal of the regulatory work.

Sometimes governments go beyond hiring people to disseminate approved messages and coerce them into doing so. Much of this occurs in commercial contexts: Employers are required to notify employees of their rights or of environmental hazards at the workplace, for example. Even though people are being forced to 'say' something they might rather not, much of this regulation is constitutionally unproblematic in the commercial context under proportionality analysis, the 'onion' model, and even a categorical approach that leaves room for a category of commercial speech subject to less constitutional protection than political speech; it is constitutionally problematic only under the inside-outside model (and, in the United States, in some decisions applying quite stringently a distinctive test for a separate category of commercial speech). One difficulty deserves mention, that the speech required by government might be mistaken for speech by

---

4 McKenna v. An Taoiseach (No. 2), [1996] 2 I.R. 10; Anderson v. City of Boston, 376 Mass. 178 (1978). The US Supreme Court declined to review the latter decision.

the commercial entities themselves. The US Supreme Court has used a sensible test on this question, though some of its applications are questionable: The government can require commercial actors to disseminate the government's statements if a reasonable observer would attribute the statements to the government and not to the entity disseminating the message.

The picture changes dramatically if the government seeks to coerce people to say things about political matters. US Supreme Court Justice Robert Jackson offered one of the most celebrated statements on this issue in holding unconstitutional a requirement that school children salute the US flag: 'If there is any fixed star in our constitutional constellation, it is that no official, high or petty, can prescribe what shall be orthodox in politics, nationalism, religion, or other matters of opinion, or force citizens to confess by word or act their faith therein.'[5] In most settings, the analysis here is simply the obverse of that of rules prohibiting people from speaking. Yet, given the possibility that some 'prescriptions' are permissible, at least in the commercial context, it becomes important to distinguish between 'matters of opinion' and other matters. Consider a seemingly simple case, a required statement about employees' rights under antidiscrimination and labor law. In the ordinary case, that the employees have such rights is not a matter of opinion. Suppose, though, that the relevant laws apply only to certain categories of workers, and the employer reasonably (though perhaps mistakenly) contends that its workers are not covered by those laws. Or, consider a required disclosure that a specific chemical is used in a workplace, a requirement imposed because the government believes that exposure to the chemical poses long-term risks to workers' health. Suppose an employer disagrees with the proposition that exposure is hazardous. Are these issues now 'matters of opinion'? The answer cannot be that the simple fact that the government requires that the statements be made removes them from the category of 'opinion'. Rather, the answer must lie in something like general social agreement that what is involved is or is not a matter of opinion.

5.5.2   Explicit subsidies

Rules about government speech lie in the background of constitutional questions about explicit subsidies to speech. As we have seen, the government can hire people to disseminate its message, and of course when

---

5 West Virginia State Board of Education v. Barnette, 319 U.S. 624 (1943).

it does so it has no obligation to hire people to disseminate competing messages. So, we must first be able to distinguish between programs that use private actors to disseminate the government's messages and those that subsidize speech in general or, as we will see, particular categories of speech. Then we must consider what limitations if any the government can place on the speech of those who receive money from it.

The answer to the first questions lies in a combination of the program's scope and, once again, social understanding. As a first approximation consider the National Orchestra of Belgium, assumed here to be heavily subsidized by the Belgian government. This is a program with a narrow scope. Though explicit discussions of the issue are understandably rare, most scholars assume that the Belgian government can exert substantial control over the Orchestra's programming: It can bar it from playing heavy metal music, for example.

Perhaps there might be an additional but loose constraint flowing from social understanding. In the present context that would be an understanding about professional concerns – perhaps musical judgment must have some role in the programming choices the government makes for the Orchestra. That constraint, though, must almost certainly be quite a loose one. Consider for example a government concerned about secessionist tendencies in the nation. Such a government might bar the Orchestra from playing music by Dutch and French composers. Notably, that restriction is motivated by an overt political judgment. The 'professionalism' constraint, if there is one, is probably something like this: The government's prescriptions must leave 'enough' professionally respectable music available to the Orchestra. We can see this as a combination of the proposition that the Orchestra's programming is the government's speech subject only to the constraints already discussed, with the proposition that restrictions that allow 'enough' music available are reasonable.

Next consider a program subsidizing a broader category of work: novels for children and young adults or traditional folk art. To use terms already introduced, these programs are clearly content-based. Few scholars think, though, that that in itself raises serious constitutional concerns. A biographer could not (and should not be able to) win a case challenging the first program as unconstitutionally discriminating against biographies, even biographies with target audiences of children and young adults. Nor could a performance artist win a lawsuit against the second program.

The rationale for these results combines several elements. The basic idea kicks in once again: Legislators might reasonably believe that the private market for children's novels and traditional folk art is too thin whereas the private market for biographies is robust enough. In addition, there is no apparent reason for thinking that legislative consideration of the scope of these programs might be infected by any identifiable problematic failure of deliberation. The spouse of the program's sponsor might write children's novels but not biographies, but that is the equivalent in this setting of the operation of normal interest group politics in shaping government programs, which, as argued in Chapter 2.1, is not enough to support a constitutional challenge. Finally, any other rule would put the legislature to something akin to an all-or-nothing choice: Support all categories of writing or art, or support none at all. No well-designed constitution would do that.

Content-based restrictions on subsidized speech, then, are constitutionally permissible. Viewpoint based ones, in contrast, are at the very least quite controversial. The core problem is this: Assume that the government has a program for subsidizing the visual arts generally. Can it refuse to award a subsidy to a photographer who proposes to take a series of photographs (staged or spontaneous) showing people burning the national flag, where the proposal meets all the remaining standards for granting a subsidy – and indeed where the proposal is, the images aside, the best of all those submitted?

We can approach an answer by considering a seemingly different problem. Can the government say to everyone who receives an arts grant, 'Because you are taking our money, you can't participate in any anti-government demonstrations'? The answer universally given in reasonably well-functioning democracies is, 'No'. The government cannot leverage its power to award money to people who qualify for it under a program's standards, to impose conditions on their actions that are unrelated to the program's purposes: The art program's purpose is to subsidize art, and the ban on demonstrating is unrelated to that purpose.

This seems obvious enough, and correct, but as usual simple formulations conceal difficulties. Here the difficulty lies in identifying the program's purpose. Recalling one of the difficulties associated with proportionality analysis, perhaps we could recharacterize the program's purpose as 'subsidizing art to the extent that doing so does not weaken the government's overall political position'. That is, we fold the limitation into the program itself. Most analysts resist this sort of recharacterization.[6] One reason may be that they take the government at its word when it describes the program as one dealing with subsidies to arts without qualification in that description. That reason could be overcome were the government explicit about the 're'-characterization from the outset. Another reason may lie, again, in social understanding: Arts programs must be about art, not politics.

Program definition, then, is the starting point. Suppose the program is defined as one supporting the arts generally, taking community sensibilities into account.[7] This is surely more viewpoint based than a program for supporting traditional folk art, but it is less viewpoint based than a program that categorically excludes depictions understood to be anti-government. Legislators might want to define the program in that way because issuing too many awards that would violate community sensibilities would undermine political support for the program, and yet might want to allow an award to a truly outstanding application that would nonetheless violate community sensibilities. Here the basic idea of deferring to reasonable legislative choices might be sufficient to uphold the program's constitutionality, though one might not implausibly describe the legislative concern about maintaining political support for the program as something distorting legislative judgment.

We come finally to the program that expressly excludes anti-government imagery and the like from eligibility for a subsidy. In a categorical framework, this seems to be a pure viewpoint-based exclusion, and constitutionally problematic for that reason. In a proportionality analysis, it seems to lack a permissible government purpose, and is constitutionally problematic at the first step in the analysis. The only nagging concern is that the subsidy program seems entirely optional constitutionally, filling in for perceived inadequacies in the private market for supporting the arts.[8] One might think that the game is not worth the candle – that private support for the arts is more desirable than government programs accompanied by quite complex statutory

---

6 The US Supreme Court did so in Agency for International Development v. Open Society International, 570 U.S. ---, 133 S. Ct. 2321 (2013).

7 This is, roughly, how the US Supreme Court treated the US arts-support program in National Endowment for the Arts v. Finley, 524 U.S. 569 (1998).

8 Government-endorsed viewpoint discrimination is almost inevitable in systems of public education. Such systems raise important questions about the role of public institutions in socializing young people, but precisely because of their focus on youth fall largely outside the domain of general free expression law.

and constitutional rules dealing with eligibility, even if (or perhaps precisely because) there will be some starving artists working away in their attics. That, though, is almost certainly a policy question, not a constitutional one.

5.6   Conclusion

This chapter has examined the way in which free expression law embodies implicit and explicit subsidies to speech.[9] In this setting free expression law brings to the surface – and brings into question – another distinction often asserted to exist between the US Constitution and constitutions elsewhere. The US Constitution, it is said, is a constitution of negative liberty, a document concerned with limiting government power over individuals, whereas many other constitutions are constitutions of positive liberty, aimed overall at ensuring that individuals are in a position to exercise their capacities as autonomous human beings. The law examined in this chapter suggests that the distinction is overdrawn, and that the US Constitution is to some extent a constitution of positive liberty as well.

---

9 In Matal v. Tam, 582 U.S. ---, 137 S. Ct. 1744 (2017), the US Supreme Court dealt with, and held unconstitutional, a limitation on an implicit subsidy indistinguishable in principle from constitutionally permissible limitations associated with explicit subsidies. It offered no explanation for the different treatment, but the decision does suggest some resistance to the idea that explicit and implicit subsidies should be treated similarly.

6 New (?) challenges

6.1 Introduction

Free expression law developed in response to publication of books and pamphlets critical of government policy (Chapter 1), and to street demonstrations and riots (Chapter 5). The law had to adapt to changing technology – daily newspapers rather than occasional pamphlets, radio and then television. But, it turned out, the basic principles developed to deal with the old problems were generally suitable to deal with the new ones. Some minor tweaks were needed, especially in schemes for licensing access to limited resources (including city streets and radio spectrum). The guiding principles and the institutional concerns that gave them structure turned out to be relatively unchanging.

Many observers believe that modern technological developments – social media and the Internet generally – have pushed us into a new era. Formulating the concerns requires some care, because the new media present several distinct problems. Regulations that are constitutionally permissible for older forms of communication may turn out to be ineffective when applied to new forms. Regulations that might be effective might also be impermissible under current understandings of free expression law. That might generate pressure to reformulate those understandings so that effective regulation can be maintained. One specific source of ineffectiveness is geographic: The new media can escape domestic regulations by 'relocating' elsewhere, in ways that newspapers cannot. The balance between the harms of speech and the benefits of allowing it might change as the scale of distribution of information changes. It might be possible to overcome old institutional constraints that structure free expression law (for example, by using international treaties rather than domestic law as the mode of regulation), but new institutional constraints might emerge. And, finally, some contend that the private actors who write the code underlying the new media effectively control what can be disseminated. Legislators representing the public might want to replace these privately generated regulations with public ones, but free expression law might stand in their way.

Because we deal here with emerging issues, we cannot describe the settled free expression law, but can only indicate some directions that law might take – how new solutions might fit into the overall structure of free expression law. One important possibility must be kept in mind throughout: The solutions to some new problems might simply be the application of existing law without significant modification.

6.2   Problems associated with geography

'The Internet has no borders', according to the Canadian Supreme Court.[1] The case in which it made that pronouncement involved the remedy for violating a company's trade secrets rights by relabeling the company's products and then selling them as the seller's own product on the seller's web-site. The Court held that the only effective remedy would require Google to 'de-index' the seller's web-site from the lists it produces for searches. Suppose, though, that Google asserts a free expression defense against de-indexing, and that an injunction against de-indexing would violate free expression as understood in US law. The Internet's characteristics would make effective regulation impossible even though such regulation is consistent with free expression as understood in Canada.

The pattern repeats itself. A French anti-racist group obtains an order from a French court against a web-site hosting an auction, operated by a person in the United States; the auction involved Nazi memorabilia, contrary to a French law against exhibiting such items.[2] Can the French court order Yahoo to make it impossible for French residents to access the auction? Suppose that for technical reasons doing so requires that the web-site install a program on its servers in the United States that will identify French users who search for the auction, and that as the right of free expression in commercial contexts is understood in the United States, prohibiting an auction of Nazi memorabilia would be unconstitutional.

The European Court of Justice has held that EU citizens have a 'right to be forgotten'. That right is understood to be of a constitutional

---

1 Google Inc. v. Equustek Solutions Inc., 2017 SCC 34.

2 Yahoo! Inc. v. LICRA, 433 F.3d 1199 (9th Cir. 2006), lays out the history of the litigation.

dimension, associated with idea of personal privacy and the right to development of the personality. The right to be forgotten gives individuals a right to demand that Internet search engines delete information about them that is outdated or irrelevant to any current matter of interest. The case itself involved a Google search done in the late 2000s that turned up newspaper articles published in 1998 saying that a Spanish businessman had had one of his properties foreclosed upon. The businessman was involved in no current controversy when the search was conducted. Google's headquarters are in the United States, where a 'right to be forgotten', understood as a right to prevent newspapers from publishing outdated personal information, would in many circumstances be unconstitutional. Can the European order be enforced against Google?

These are problems where the extraterritorial application of domestic legal rules consistent with domestic interpretations of principles of free expression might be unconstitutional under some other nation's interpretation of those same principles. Such problems did not arise only after the development of the Internet. A Canadian injunction against publishing details about a lurid crime was ineffective because those same details were published in US newspapers and broadcast over US radio and television stations easily accessible within Canada. A British effort to prevent the publication of *Spycatcher*, a memoir by a British spy, was rendered ineffective by the book's publication in Australia.

The United States, with its distinctive free expression regime, has addressed – or perhaps exacerbated – some of these problems through statutes influenced by US constitutional considerations. A US court blocked the enforcement of the de-indexing judgment, invoking ill-defined constitutional considerations and a statute immunizing Internet intermediaries such as Google from various forms of liability as equitable considerations weighing against enforcement. A federal statute, known by its acronym as the SPEECH Act, prohibits enforcement in US courts of foreign libel judgments that would violate the constitutional standards applied to libelous statements in the United States.[3]

---

3 Yahoo's attempt to obtain an injunction against enforcing the Nazi memorabilia judgment was dismissed because some judges concluded that the United States did not have jurisdiction over the French organization that obtained the judgment in France, and because other judges con-

How should the legal system deal with these problems? Note the formulation: The question is about the legal system as a whole, not free expression law. For, in the end, most of the problems arise from international law.

The first question is whether the domestic legal rule – Canadian trade secret law or the French rule against selling Nazi memorabilia – has extraterritorial legal effect (from the perspective of the domestic jurisdiction, Canada or France). The next question is whether the second jurisdiction's domestic law (in the examples, the United States) recognizes whatever extraterritorial effect there might be. In the first instance that is a question of international law.

Suppose that the legal rule is intended to have extraterritorial effect and that the second jurisdiction would ordinarily give it such effect. But suppose, as in the examples, that the second jurisdiction – again, the United States – would hold the legal rule unconstitutional were it applied in an entirely local dispute. The extent to which that should affect the analysis of the problems is here a question of general constitutional law. A legal system might treat unconstitutionality under domestic law as dispositive against the foreign judgment, or it might take that unconstitutionality to be relevant but not dispositive – for example, if the foreign rule was quite important to the foreign nation and the infringement on free expression as understood in the second jurisdiction relatively small (if the second jurisdiction's system has a concept of small infringements available to it, for example through the onion model).

Treaties might address some of these and similar problems, though they can eliminate them entirely only if we make some assumptions about the role of treaties within domestic legal systems. Consider an international treaty obligating signatories to enforce libel judgments found constitutionally permissible by the highest court in the jurisdiction entering them. It is a question of domestic constitutional law, whether a treaty can override otherwise applicable constitutional rules, or whether the existence of an international treaty should influence how a domestic court interprets domestic principles of free expression.

These problems of geographical application of rules found consistent by one jurisdiction with its understanding of free expression are

---

cluded that the free expression issues were not ready for decision prior to any attempt to enforce the French judgment in the United States.

serious ones, but their solution, if there is one, lies in principles of international law and general constitutional law, not in free expression law.

6.3   Problems associated with scale

The Internet transformed the pornography industry. Material that would be obscene in some US jurisdictions – and that therefore could be banned in those jurisdiction – became available everywhere. Effective enforcement of constitutionally permissible regulations of obscene materials became impossible because the Internet vastly increased its distribution and put its producers and distributors out of reach of jurisdictions that wished to – and permissibly could – regulate it. Here scale and geography interact.

Another widely discussed problem is that of 'Internet trolls'. Trolls come in various guises, but the core free expression issue arises in this way: A person makes a statement about some issue of public policy; people use social media to comment critically on the statement; some of those criticisms take the form of seeming threats to physically harm the initial speaker; and those threats come to the speaker's attention. Another important variant blends the political with the personal: A man vents his frustration about how the police or the courts have treated him in connection with a domestic dispute by using strong language amounting to a threat against the police, the judge, his partner, and her lawyers. The existence of social media may loosen conventional constraints on expression, so that people who would be reluctant to make threats face-to-face or even in a letter are less reluctant to do so over the Internet.

Free expression law has a reasonably well-settled approach to threats. Threats cause various harms that legislatures can address: Targets sometimes take steps to reduce the possibility that the threat will succeed (by hiding, hiring security guards, and the like), they suffer the psychological harm of being placed in fear, and their 'quiet repose' – as the common law tradition puts it – is disturbed. Yet, discourse about public matters often contains what the US Supreme Court called 'political hyperbole'. The Court made that observation about a statement made during a discussion of police brutality and compulsory military service by a small group of young men: 'If they ever make me carry a rifle the first man I want to get in my sights is LBJ [US President

Lyndon Baines Johnson].'[4] We must therefore distinguish between 'mere' political hyperbole and 'true threats'.

There are several candidates for identifying a true threat. One is subjective and focuses on the person making the threat: Did that person intend to carry it out when the circumstances for doing so presented themselves? Another is subjective and focuses on the target: Was she actually put in fear when she learned that the threat had been made? A third is objective: Would a reasonable target be placed in fear upon learning of the threat? As a matter of statutory interpretation the US Supreme Court held that a federal statute dealing with threats adopts the speaker-focused subjective standard.[5] That standard does not give the target's reaction – the fear that is one of the harms that liability for threats is aimed at – as much weight as the other standards do.

We can choose among the possible standards by thinking about each one's chilling effect. The underlying concern is that the rule we adopt might impose a cost on free expression by punishing and deterring mere hyperbole. The target-focused subjective standard allows liability to be imposed when an unusually sensitive target experiences fear when most other people would not. We might say that this standard gives the target something close to a veto over what others can say (in the context of making statements on the border between hyperbole and true threats) and so is likely to have the largest chilling effect. The difficulty with other standards is slightly different, akin to the difficulty with libel law discussed in Chapter 2.2. The concern is that the ultimate decision-maker on liability – in the US setting, a jury – will mistakenly find that a speaker who merely intended to make a hyperbolic statement actually intended to carry out the threat, or will mistakenly find that a reasonable person would be placed in fear upon learning of what is actually only a hyperbolic statement.

Notably, *all* the standards pose the risk of mistakenly imposing liability for merely hyperbolic statements. But, in light of the fact that the harms imposed by true threats are serious ones, legislatures can reasonably choose to penalize true threats notwithstanding the fact that doing so will chill some merely hyperbolic statements. The question is about the amount of chill, and once again the 'basic idea' presented in Chapter 1.2.1 should guide the development of free expression law: Has the

---

4 Watts v. United States, 394 U.S. 705 (1969).
5 Elonis v. United States, 575 U.S. ---, 135 S. Ct. 2001 (2015).

legislature chosen a reasonable standard? One might contend with some force that the target-focused subjective standard is unreasonable because of the power it gives to especially sensitive targets. But, both the speaker-focused subjective standard and the objective standard appear to be quite reasonable, and whichever the legislature chooses satisfies the requirements of free expression law. Or, put another way, the US Supreme Court was correct in seeing that the real questions about threat liability involve statutory interpretation, not free expression law. Importantly for the present discussion, nothing in the preceding analysis turns on the fact that Internet trolls operate over the Internet: Here technological change alters the scale of the problem but not the analytic framework we use to address the problem.

Threats that disturb quiet repose without inducing fear are probably best understood as invasions of privacy. 'Revenge porn' presents a similar issue, which in the Internet context once again raises issues of scale. Revenge porn consists of revealing photographs taken before a couple separated, then distributed to embarrass the person depicted, as revenge for (typically) her actions in breaking off the relationship. In form this is a simple problem of invasion of privacy, and we know how to analyze laws imposing liability for invasion of privacy; depending on the underlying law, they pose rights-versus-rights or rights-versus-interests conflicts.

Is a law imposing liability for distributing revenge porn different from a standard invasion of privacy law? Proposals for such laws begin with the observation that revenge porn is primarily a phenomenon of distribution through social media. Standard invasion of privacy laws, in contrast, allow for liability quite broadly, but raise interesting free expression questions almost exclusively when a newspaper or magazine publishes something that is alleged to invade privacy. But, notably, the newspaper acts as a screening agent, invoking some sort of 'newsworthiness' standard in choosing to publish. In contrast, there is no similar screening agency for revenge porn. Further, the use of social media for distribution means that revenge porn is more likely to reach viewers who know the person depicted, indicating that the invasion of privacy may be particularly serious; diminishing a person's stature in the eyes of her friends may be more harmful to her than diminishing her status among the public generally, who might not even know who she is. And, finally, the social media may simply reach many more people than newspapers and magazines. The latter two reasons suggest that the harms inflicted by revenge porn are of significantly larger scale than occur in traditional invasion of privacy cases.

It would be relatively easy to find a revenge porn statute constitutionally permissible under a balancing or proportionality analysis. We would start with a traditional invasion of privacy law. There are several variants. A jurisdiction might hold that, on balance, imposing liability on newspapers or magazines for invasion of privacy for publishing what they regard as newsworthy material impairs free expression more than it protects personal privacy. Or, it might allow liability but only when the courts determine that the material was not newsworthy. Or, of course, it might allow liability quite generally, finding that invasions of privacy typically outweigh the public benefit of publishing intrusive material. With revenge porn, there is no 'newsworthiness' screen at all, suggesting that it would be easy to find the infringement of free expression rights relatively small (impairing only the free expression rights of individuals unconnected to the distribution of material of interest to a wide audience). And, it would similarly be relatively easy to find that the intrusion on privacy is likely to be relatively large, given the sexually charged nature of the pictures distributed.

In a more categorical system, the analysis might track that outlined earlier for statutes punishing dissemination of specific false statements (Chapter 2.2): A legislature that adopts a revenge porn statute implicitly (or perhaps even explicitly) rejects autonomy-based justifications for free expression, so the fact that the distributor's self-determined expression is impaired is irrelevant in light of the basic idea of deference applied to reasonable legislative choices among theories of free expression. Revenge porn does little to promote truth or advance democratic decision-making. One might conclude that a revenge porn statute should be constitutionally permissible. (The same result might be reached by carving out an exception for revenge porn – based on the absence of a 'newsworthiness' screen and the greater scale of harm – even in jurisdictions that find liability for invasion of privacy generally impermissible.)

Yet, we know enough about how people use existing doctrinal structures to deal with new problems to know that both balancing and categorical analysis might lead courts to find revenge porn statutes inconsistent with freedom of expression: They might not think the harm especially great, or might think that the problem is no different from the one posed by traditional invasion of privacy liability, which they have already concluded is inconsistent with free expression.

On their surface the problems posed by Internet trolls and revenge porn fit reasonably well within established components of free expression law: They are threats and invasions of privacy. The German 'social media' law with which we began suggests, though, that technology complicates the problems. In prior eras it was relatively easy for a target to know who was threatening her or invading her privacy. But, as the famous cartoon has it, 'On the Internet, nobody knows you're a dog.' That is, speakers using social media can rather easily conceal their identities. So, a rule that imposes liability only on the person using the Internet to make a threat or invade privacy might not be as effective as such a rule applied to traditional media.

We can come up with various procedural 'fixes' to reduce the problems posed by anonymity, such as enabling targets to get information from intermediaries – 'platform' operators like Facebook – about who put the information on the platform. Such procedural devices raise no substantial free expression issues. That cannot be said of laws, like the German one, that impose liability under some circumstances on the intermediaries themselves.

Consider a statute imposing liability on an intermediary for disseminating a threat. That liability will induce the intermediary to screen material submitted for dissemination to determine whether it is a threat. And, whether the threat standard is objective or subjective, the intermediary will inevitably prevent the distribution of material that is *not* a threat. This is liability's chilling effect once again. Free expression law is generally structured so as to reduce chilling effects. The German statute takes one approach: impose liability not for disseminating the material, but for failing to have a system in place for determining whether the material is a threat. That approach will have some chilling effect, because such a system will (again inevitably) identify some statements as threats that are not true threats, again under either the objective or subjective standard. But, the mere fact that the intermediary disseminates something later determined to be a true threat would not be in itself a basis for liability.

We can readily come up with rules that protect intermediaries even more substantially: liability for recklessly distributing a threat, or liability for distributing a threat after having been notified by the target of the existence of prior threats, or liability for distributing what the intermediary knows to be a threat. Once again, whether these rules are consistent with free expression principles rests almost entirely on answers to questions about how substantial each one's chilling effect is. And, at some point, free expression law will have to accept legislative judgments about the chilling effect's size.

Recent elections in several nations have raised yet another new version of an old problem. Some campaign finance regulation rests on the proposition that voters are receiving too much information from one side, not enough from the other. Phrased in terms of imbalance, the concern is about leveling the playing field. There is, though, another way to describe the problem: Voters have limited time and attention to devote to politics, and they can be overwhelmed by the sheer volume of material that is sent their way. Sheer repetition affects the view voters take of some issues and candidates, a 'distortion' of deliberation that goes beyond the usual impact that emotion has upon reason.

As a general matter, if we center regulation around the listeners' perspective (Chapter 3.4.2), we can devise regulations that deal with the problem of information flooding in a familiar conceptual structure. And, as usual, the Internet adds a layer of complication.

To begin, is the harm of information-overload one that the government can permissibly address? The justification for regulating it is unabashedly paternalist: In the legislature's view people are unable to determine for themselves when they have heard enough about some issue or candidate that they can turn away from additional efforts to say the same thing to them. And paternalism, we might think, is not a permissible basis for regulating information – that is, even if paternalism is permissible in other domains, its premises are inconsistent with the ideas underlying free expression.

The anti-paternalist objection is overstated. Paternalist regulation of information is common even in speaker-focused systems of free expression law. Governments require producers of potentially harmful products to disclose information about the harms even though potential consumers could discover that information on their own. Even more, governments can ban harmful products rather than allow them to be sold with full disclosure of the potential harms, on the theory that potential buyers are likely to misunderstand the disclosures for well-known reasons such as a systematic tendency to underestimate the importance of small risks and an 'optimism bias' that leads everyone to think that, though someone is going to be harmed by the product, he or she will not be among the unlucky ones.

Further, paternalism is closely associated with listener-focused accounts of free expression law. To return to Meiklejohn's words, if what really matters is that everything worth saying be said, the legislature has to be allowed to determine not only what is worth saying but, more importantly, the point at which everything worth saying has been said. 'You've heard enough' is precisely what a listener-focused account allows the government to say.

Finally, recall that the basic idea underlying free expression law encompasses the idea that legislatures can choose among reasonable political theories as justifications for the regulations they enact. Although a fully general paternalism might not be a reasonable political theory (because it might authorize complete displacement of individual choices across the board by the views of some dictator, benevolent or otherwise), a political theory that allows for discrete exercises of paternalism is almost certainly a reasonable one.

Legislatures can choose to treat the harm of information flooding as worth addressing. If we find the person doing the flooding, imposing liability is straight-forward. The more interesting problem involves someone who encourages others to flood social media with information. Could a legislature disqualify candidates for office who encourage their supporters to retweet their messages, or to 'like' other social media messages, where there is a real possibility that such encouragement will lead to information flooding?

A first analogy might be to standard ideas about aiding and abetting, or being an accessory to conduct the legislature can treat as harmful. (The terminology does not matter: 'aiding and abetting', 'accessorial liability', 'facilitating unlawful action' – all can be used to identify the underlying approach.) Among those ideas are so-called mental elements: 'intent' that specific listeners – or perhaps a small subset of listeners – engage in information flooding; 'knowledge' that some listeners will do so; or 'recklessness' about whether information flooding will result from the candidate's statements. The looser the required mental element, the larger the effect on deterring – chilling, once again – candidate speech.

Another important idea is 'proximity to success'. The person who sells ink to someone who publishes prohibited obscene materials has enabled the unlawful action, but it would be absurd – and inconsistent with any sensible account of free expression – to allow the legislature to treat the ink-seller as an accessory to publishing obscenity. Similarly with someone who sells computers to people who engage in information flooding. In other settings we treat the question of proximity as one of degree, leaving it to ultimate decision-makers such as juries or, here, those in charge of determining who qualifies for placement on the ballot to decide whether the candidate's actions are close enough to information flooding. And, as we saw in connection with the jury's role in determining whether political speech is closely connected enough to unlawful action (Chapter 1.5.2), here too we might worry about unconsciously biased decision-makers who might find, for example, that insurgent political candidates are close enough to information flooding while more traditional ones are not.

As already noted, concerns about chilling effects are important here. We might well worry about taking the view that free expression law allows the imposing of liability on anyone who aids and abets *any* form of unlawful speech, even if aiding and abetting is defined to require one of the stricter mental elements and a finding of proximity to the unlawful action. The breadth of such potential liability might have a substantial chilling effect on many types of speech. We might, though, allow for more targeted versions of aiding and abetting liability. Doctrinally we would require the legislature to take a more narrowly tailored approach (the US formulation) or adopt a less restrictive means (the proportionality formulation sometimes echoed in US doctrine). Perhaps it would be permissible for a legislature to identify information flooding as a particular problem to which aiding and abetting liability would attach. Or, perhaps the legislature could identify specific forms of encouragement that are especially likely to lead to information flooding.

Of course if it is enough that the legislature identify 'information flooding' as a specific problem as to which aiding and abetting liability can attach, in principle it could identify other harms to which aiding and abetting liability could attach: All that would be prohibited is invoking the general law of aiding and abetting no matter what the underlying harm. This presents another facet of the basic idea about deference to reasonable legislative choices. Here, the question would be: Do we trust legislatures to impose aiding and abetting liability only where doing so is a reasonable way of addressing a relatively narrow or well-defined harm?

All these problems have a similar structure: New technologies make available new versions of old problems. The new versions operate on a different scale from the old ones. Sometimes scale does not matter, and the solutions free expression law has reached for the old problems are suitable for the new ones; the law dealing with threats might be sufficient to deal with Internet trolls, for example. Sometimes scale matters somewhat, and tinkering with existing solutions might be sufficient, preserving the core of the old solutions while modifying some peripheral features. Perhaps unfortunately, though, sometimes quantity turns into quality: The problem on a large scale is quite different from the analogous small-scale problem. Then the questions are two: How can we tell that the scale of the new problem makes it truly different from the old, only seemingly similar, problem? And, once we do, how can we deal with the new problem? These are among the most important questions on the horizon.

6.4   Problems associated with private control of important media

In 2010 Facebook supported a social-science experiment that manipulated information provided to users by Facebook, to determine whether that information could increase turn-out on election day. (It could.) In 2016 former Facebook employees charged that the company manipulated the section of the site that told users what was 'trending' to downplay trends favoring conservatives. (Facebook denied that it had done so, but apparently did modify its internal practices in response to the criticism.) Put those two observations together, and we can see how Facebook might manipulate what its users saw not to increase turn-out overall, but to increase turn-out by voters who supported candidates Facebook's owners favored: Give the turn-out promoting information only to people a Facebook algorithm identifies as likely to support Facebook-preferred candidates.

Facebook, Twitter, Google – all dominate segments of the social media economy in the way that some manufacturers used to dominate segments of the traditional economy. Their owners can exploit that dominance to their own ends – or, unless the owners themselves intervene, third parties can do so. And, because those companies operate in the domain of information, some scholars have suggested that something should be done to reduce the risk that they can exercise an undesirable amount of political influence: Invoke ideas akin to those deployed in antitrust law to break these companies up, or impose duties on them akin to those imposed on public utilities that, for technical reasons, necessarily held local monopolies.

This too may be only a modern manifestation of an old problem. The media critic A.J. Liebling wrote in 1960: 'Freedom of the press is guaranteed only to those who own one.' Is the control Google and Facebook have over the codes their employees write different from the control newspaper owners have over the editorial content of their papers? Here too scale might matter. Historically, some newspapers had monopolies in their cities, and more do so today – but, of course, the overall media environment is quite competitive. The major private actors on the Internet might have enough control over some aspects of information distribution to lead legislators to search for methods to regulate them 'in the public interest' – and, as the 'social network' statute described in Chapter 1 suggests, perhaps the search is a reasonable one. Are there paths open to (reasonable) regulation of these companies that are consistent with free expression law?

According to the US Supreme Court, newspapers have 'no special immunity from the application of general laws', including antitrust laws.[6] One such general law is contract law. Facebook and Twitter offer potential users 'terms of service' that define what users can post (Facebook's users can post only under their real names, for example, and Twitter's users should not post nudity) and, importantly, what Facebook and Twitter can do (both have provisions dealing with what the companies can do with information users provide, including provisions about sharing the information with other companies). The companies offer these terms on a 'take it or leave it' basis, and – given the firms' domination of the markets within which they operate – they are almost certainly contracts of adhesion. As a matter of general contract law, the government has the power to regulate terms in contracts of adhesion – and, indeed, even terms in ordinary contracts.

Perhaps, then, the general law of contract could be invoked to prevent Facebook and Twitter from using information they acquire from their users in political experiments or, more broadly, as the basis for sending messages to users that the companies select or as the basis for blocking messages users try to send. In 2016, for example, the US Congress enacted the Consumer Review Fairness Act. The Act made it illegal for a company to insert provisions in its contracts with consumers that limit the consumers' ability to review the company's products. On its face the Act only prohibits Amazon from blocking reviews of Amazon, not reviews of products sold on Amazon. Suppose, though, that the Act swept more broadly and limited Facebook's power to limit reviews posted on Facebook.

---

6 Associated Press v. NLRB, 301 U.S. 103 (1937).

On the face of things, such a regulation would be information-specific or, in traditional free expression terms, content-based. As such, it might have to be justified by very strong reasons: The government might have to show a close causal connection between limiting the companies' ability to choose which messages to spread and some important government interest, and doing so might well be quite difficult. These regulations could be treated as 'general laws' if we could identify rules about what can and cannot be included in contracts of adhesion that are even roughly analogous, and, again, it is unclear that there are such rules.

Perhaps, though, contract law deployed on users' behalf might accomplish something. What of antitrust law? Justice Hugo Black argued that the First Amendment *supported* applying antitrust law to newspapers:

> That Amendment rests on the assumption that the widest possible dissemination of information from diverse and antagonistic sources is essential to the welfare of the public, that a free press is a condition of a free society. Surely a command that the government itself shall not impede the free flow of ideas does not afford non-governmental combinations a refuge if they impose restraints upon that constitutionally guaranteed freedom.[7]

That statement might well be overbroad. Even at its broadest, though, it suggests only that we should treat newspapers, Facebook, and Twitter just as we would treat a government when it decided what messages to send out, and, as we have seen, the law of government speech would give them wide discretion (Chapter 5.5.1). That does not seem to be what those concerned about the excessive power of social media giants want, though.

Treating antitrust law as 'general' means applying ordinary antitrust principles to Facebook, Twitter, and Google. So, for example, if a nation's antitrust law allows the government to break up companies simply because they are 'too large', that principle could be invoked against them. But, when France sought to limit the growth of media empires – newspapers moving into broadcast media – with a specific law on press expansion, the French Constitutional Council objected. Expansion could be limited if the newspapers engaged in various bad tactics that helped them expand, but not if their growth resulted from 'natural' forces, meaning from uncoerced consumer choices.[8]

---

7 Associated Press v. United States, 326 U.S. 1 (1945).
8 Constitutional Council, Decision 84–181 on press concentration.

This identifies two sources of difficulty. First, drafting a press- or social media-specific 'antitrust' law that can be treated as a general law might well be so difficult as to be impossible in practice. The argument would have to be that the principles used to attack overly large Internet companies are already embedded in other antitrust laws and are merely being tweaked to deal with the special problems presented by large social media organizations. We might fairly doubt that such an argument would be even plausible.

Second, today's large Internet companies may have achieved their size by 'natural' growth: They may have succeeded because they have provided users with a better product than their rivals, as consumers see it. This is clearest in the case of Google, less so with true social media companies. Google's domination of the market for search engines does not prevent anyone else from coming up with a better search engine. Facebook and Twitter are different because they provide 'network' services; that is, the benefits a new user gets from signing up flow from the fact that lots and lots of people have already signed up. Antitrust law is not a good response to the size of such services; public utility type regulation is more promising.

Before turning to that topic, one cautionary note. The world of social media is quite young. Facebook was launched in the mid-2000s and took off around 2010. Twitter began a little later, and expanded rapidly a bit sooner. Even the 'network' characterization of Facebook and Twitter can be challenged: Alternatives or supplements such as Instagram and Tumblr have grown (by some measures Instagram is 'bigger' than Twitter). The history of social media is one of surges and declines of specific modes and, even more, companies. The literature on social media is filled with comments like, 'Remember My Space and Ask Jeeves' – companies that soared into prominence then receded into the background, or even disappeared. Today we are apparently experiencing a substantial decline in the role of blogs, which were displaced by Facebook posts – and now, it may be that Facebook posts are being replaced by Twitter feeds. Perhaps, then, we should hold our breath and see what happens rather than develop regulations and attempt to fit them into, or modify, free expression law.

6.4.1   Public utility regulation

Governments regulate privately owned suppliers of electricity, telephone services, water, and more under the heading of 'public utilities'.

Some of the ideas associated with public utility regulation might be deployed in regulating large Internet entities like Facebook and Google. The constitutional question is not whether such entities are exactly the same as the public utilities governments have regulated, but is instead whether they are enough like traditional public utilities that ideas and policies associated with public utility regulation can help us devise – and then analyze under free expression law – Internet regulations.

Traditional public utilities have several characteristics. They provide people with important goods, as the list just given indicates. Because of their economic characteristics – generally described as 'economies of scale', meaning roughly that the more people they supply, the cheaper it is to provide each additional increment of the goods – they tend toward monopoly or near-monopoly. Facebook does not have economies of scale in that sense; indeed almost no Internet service transmitting information from one place to another does because once the information is available it costs almost nothing to send it to one, two, or a million people. But, Facebook and Twitter have something similar: The more people using each service, the more valuable it is to other potential users. Whether search engines like Google are like public utilities is more questionable. They provide an important service, but there appears to be nothing other than good design that makes Google a better search engine than Bing or DuckDuckGo (if indeed it is a better search engine).

The core of traditional public utility regulation couples two elements: A common-carrier obligation, which requires utilities to provide service to all who seek it, and price regulation, typically a requirement that the utility charge the same price to everyone in a well-defined class of users. Here the analogy to Internet service providers is clear: In principle a government could require that every Internet service provider offer its services to everyone at the same cost, a policy sometimes referred to generically as 'net neutrality'. Invoking the idea of 'general' laws, the government could also allow or prescribe different rates for different categories of users where the categories were defined by, for example, the amount of use: Internet service providers could be allowed to charge heavy users higher prices than those who use the service less often. These are policy choices that ordinarily would raise no free expression concerns.

What about categories defined by the content of what is being transmitted? During the US election season, the (regulated) television industry is required to sell time for political advertisements at a lower cost than commercial users are charged. Cable television systems, which are less heavily regulated, nonetheless can be required to carry local television programs in addition to national ones, and to make some channels available for 'public access', which is like walk-in programming by members of the general public. The US Supreme Court has upheld these regulations against challenges based on the First Amendment, in a series of confusing and divided opinions that probably can best be understood as applying a reasonableness test with a bit of skepticism thrown in.

It might be, then, that net neutrality coupled with modest preferences for some kinds of expression and perhaps some modest disadvantages for other kinds are consistent with free expression law. If so, the reason is, once again, that there appear to be no obvious institutional biases – other than those flowing from ordinary pluralist politics – at work.

Facebook and Twitter have some similarities to traditional public utilities. Yet, the concerns people express about Facebook and Twitter are, in some ways, the flip side of concerns associated with traditional public utilities. There we are worried about discrimination against users – a failure to make electricity service available, for example. With Facebook and Twitter people worry about policies that make them *too* available, for cyberstalking, cyberbullying, dissemination of fake news, and the like. *Allowing* Facebook and Twitter to exclude users who cyberstalk (and the like) is entirely consistent with traditional public utilities law, which consists of powers available to governments that they need not exercise to their fullest extent. Ideas rooted in public utilities law probably have no purchase with respect to regulations like the social media statute introduced in Chapter 1, or proposals to require Facebook to screen posts for cyberstalking or fake news. Such regulations must be analyzed using the other principles embedded in free expression law.

6.4.2   Regulating code

The problems discussed in this section arise from problems some observers see in how privately owned companies might act. A famous phrase by Larry Lessig captures the underlying idea: Code as Law. That is, the decisions Facebook, Twitter, and Google make function in practical terms to structure people's lives in ways not readily distinguishable from the way that the law does. If we think – as we do – that we the people, acting through elections, should control those who make law, Lessig suggests, we should think that we should be able to control those who write code, at least where the code-writers exercise power similar in scope to that exercised by our law-makers. The idea, that is, is that just as there is democratic control of legislatures there should be democratic control of powerful Internet entities.

The difficulty, of course, is that we control law-makers in two ways – through elections and through constitutional limits on their power, including free expression law. Writing code is expression. (Technically one might contend that code is simply a language like Spanish: People who know code can look at a page of code and understand what it says and does. Or, one might treat code as expression because the things we are concerned about – manipulation of the information Facebook provides and the like – are expression in the ordinary sense.) So, any law we might enact to control powerful Internet entities based on the idea that they are effectively law-makers when they write code, must satisfy free expression law's requirements.

Perhaps, though, the problem here is akin to the problems posed by campaign finance regulation. Campaign finance regulations are said to be in the service of democracy itself, in a way that regulation of speech causing unlawful action is not (except in the quite indirect sense that the action is unlawful as a result of democratic decisions to make it so). So too are regulations of powerful Internet entities: They are democratically developed regulations aimed at promoting democracy. As we saw, we might have misgivings about whether campaign finance regulations rest on a truly disinterested assessment of what best promotes democracy (Chapter 3.4.2). It is not clear that similar misgivings should attend regulations of powerful Internet entities. And, as we also saw, the misgivings associated with campaign finance regulations might not be strong enough to rebut the deference recommended by the basic analysis. Similarly, perhaps, with Internet regulations: We should defer to reasonable legislative judgments that one or another regulation does promote democracy.

6.5   Conclusion

As we have seen, proportionality analysis might seem to provide an easy fix for new problems because it seems to allow modest tweaks at one or another step, just enough to deal with the problem at hand:

Increase the scale of the harm, and a regulation whose adverse impact on speech was previously disproportionate might become proportionate, for example. From the other direction, issues of scale might lead judges in more categorical systems to tweak the categories modestly, as US judges did in introducing the category of child pornography.

As before, the distinction between proportionality and categorical approaches may narrow as new problems present themselves. Put another way: Existing structures of legal doctrine may be completely adequate to deal with emerging problems of free expression law.

Conclusion

We have examined the law of free expression in contexts of reasonably well-functioning democracies. The twenty-first century has brought not only new technological challenges, examined in Chapter 6, but also new political ones – in particular, a widespread concern with the possibility of democratic backsliding. Democracies backslide when they move from functioning reasonably well to functioning badly – or not at all, as when politics makes it impossible for legislatures to enact legislation that all agree is important – with the end-point being a transition from democracy to mild or severe authoritarian rule. Recent examples of democratic backsliding may have been facilitated by some of the technological developments we have considered, as charismatic proto-authoritarian leaders utilize social media to bypass existing political parties and other gatekeepers of democracy.

We have known for a long time that democracy itself can lead to democratic decline. Philosopher Karl Popper used the term 'paradox of liberal tolerance' – tolerance of the intolerant – in 1945 to describe the problem that liberal societies seem to be committed to tolerating views whose adoption would produce illiberal polities. Every reasonably well-functioning democracy has political parties with anti-democratic programs. If things go reasonably well those parties remain on the fringes, gaining a handful of votes and at most a few seats in legislatures.

Things do not always go well, though, and these parties can move from the fringes to the center of politics, raising the possibility of backsliding. At least since the middle of the twentieth century constitutionalists have known that the best thing to do about these parties is to nip them in the bud: If conditions favor their growth, deny them access to the ballot box and take other actions that allow their supporters to voice their views but impede their ability to implement them through ordinary legislative politics. Reflecting in 1937 on the rise of fascism in Europe, political theorist Karl Lowenstein called this 'militant democracy', a democracy militant in its own defense. The difficulty with militant democracy is that, as one account has it, it requires the adoption of 'pre-emptive, prima facie illiberal measures'.[1] One facet of their illiberalism is their inconsistency with well-established components of free expression law.

Militant democracy leads to the exclusion from ballots of political parties precisely because of their programs – a nearly pristine example of a penalty based on content. It is dramatically different from other bases for exclusion from the ballot, such as failure to demonstrate some minimum level of popular support, a requirement justified by a content-neutral concern to avoid making ballots too confusing for voters. The penalty is not as severe as criminal prosecution for holding anti-democratic views, which might matter were the appropriate test proportionality or some sort of balancing. But, for political parties ballot exclusion is something like a death sentence – indeed, that is pretty much its point. Further, militant democracy's measures are likely to be most effective when an anti-democratic party has appeared on the scene but has not grown too large to escape control by law. So, precisely at the point that militant democracy's measures might be invoked most effectively, it might well be the case that even a 'mere' ballot exclusion would be disproportionate to the threat at that time.

Today the threat that militant democracy might have to deal with is 'fake news', the dissemination of falsehoods with the aim – and sometimes with the effect – of undermining public confidence in democratic institutions. How our institutions of free expression could respond to this threat is unclear. A government agency authorized to certify news as fake or true would certainly have a chilling effect, and would be open to obvious political manipulation: Messages that confirm the 'establishment's' views would be certified as true, those outside the establishment certified as fake. And, presumably, those who spread fake news would seek to undermine the agency's credibility.

Perhaps, then, militant democracy cannot be reconciled with the general body of free expression law. Unlike many other laws, such as those dealing with social welfare policy, though, militant democracy operates within free expression's domain. Perhaps we must accept that militant democracy is incompatible with free expression law. We then have two paths. We could treat militant democracy as unconstitutional – not

---

1 Jan-Werner Müller, 'Militant Democracy', in Oxford Handbook of Comparative Constitutional Law (Michel Rosenfeld and András Sajó eds., Oxford: Oxford University Press, 2012).

merely 'prima facie illiberal', but completely illiberal – and hope that polities are strong enough to resist backsliding. (We might think as well that militant democracy is unlikely to stop democratic backsliding in those nations susceptible to it.) This appears to be the path preferred by most US scholars of free expression.

Alternatively, we might treat militant democracy as a necessary exception to general free expression law. Then, though, we might wonder about the possibility of creating other exceptions – and about how we could develop a standard of 'necessity' that would prevent general free expression law from becoming riddled with exceptions. Perhaps because of a division of academic labor, with some scholars concerned with how constitutional design can support stable democracy and others concerned with free expression law, we have very little to go on here.

There may be many paradoxes of free expression, or at least real tensions within the domain of free expression, but the paradox of militant democracy may be the one requiring the most urgent attention today.

References

Ash, Timothy Garton. Free Speech: Ten Principles for a Connected World (New Haven: Yale University Press, 2016)

Ferejohn, John A. and William Eskridge. A Republic of Statutes: The New American Constitution (Princeton: Yale University Press, 2010)

Issacharoff, Samuel. Fragile Democracies: Contested Power in the Era of Constitutional Courts (New York: Cambridge University Press, 2015)

Meiklejohn, Alexander. Free Speech and its Relation to Self-Government (Clark, NJ: The Lawbook Exchange Ltd., 1948)

Meiklejohn, Alexander. 'Free Speech Is an Absolute', 1961 Supreme Court Review 245 (1961)

Müller, Jan-Werner. 'Militant Democracy', in Oxford Handbook of Comparative Constitutional Law (Michel Rosenfeld and András Sajó eds., Oxford: Oxford University Press, 2012)

Schauer, Frederick. 'Rights, Constitutions, and the Perils of Panglossism', 38 Oxford Journal of Legal Studies (forthcoming 2018)

Stacey, Richard. 'The Magnetism of Moral Reasoning and the Principle of Proportionality in Comparative Constitutional Adjudication', American Journal of Comparative Law (forthcoming 2018)

Tushnet, Mark, Joseph Blocher, and Alan Chen. Free Speech beyond Words: The Surprising Reach of the First Amendment (New York: New York University Press, 2017)

Waldron, Jeremy. The Harm in Hate Speech (Cambridge, MA: Harvard University Press, 2012)

Waldron, Jeremy. 'Heckle: To Disconcert with Questions, Challenges, or Gibes' 2017 Supreme Court Review 1 (2017)

Index

Titles in the **Elgar Advanced Introductions** series include: